MR. ONLINE'S
Playbook

MR. ONLINE'S Playbook

125 PRO TIPS FOR ONLINE QUALITATIVE PROJECTS

JEFF WALKOWSKI

Paramount Market Publishing, Inc.

Paramount Market Publishing, Inc.
274 North Goodman Street, STE D-214
Rochester, NY 14607
www.paramountbooks.com
Phone: 607-275-8100

Publisher: James Madden
Editorial Director: Doris Walsh

Copyright © 2023 Jeff Walkowski

All rights reserved. No part of this book may be reproduced, stored in a retrieval system, or transmitted in any form or by any means, electronic, mechanical, photocopying, recording, or otherwise, without the prior written permission of the publisher. Further information may be obtained from Paramount Market Publishing, Inc., 274 North Goodman Street, STE D-214, Rochester, NY 14607.

This publication is designed to provide accurate and authoritative information in regard to the subject matter covered. It is sold with the understanding that the publisher is not engaged in rendering legal, accounting, or other professional services. If legal advice or other expert assistance is required, the services of a competent professional should be sought.

All trademarks are the property of their respective companies.

ISBN 13: 978-1-941688-82-3 | ISBN 10: 1-941688-82-9

Contents

Foreword *by Casey Sweet*   vii

Preface   xi

Acknowledgments   xiii

Section 1 The Fundamentals   1

Section 2 Selling Online Qualitative   24

Section 3 General Design Considerations   35

Section 4 Recruitment   51

Section 5 Discussion Guides   65

Section 6 Observer Management   104

Section 7 Moderation   108

Section 8 Analysis   146

Mr. Online's Tipsheet   153

About the Author   163

Foreword

Thirty years ago, who knew that we would now be living in a world where being connected to the internet is woven into our daily lives— some might say "our very being." Back then, we conducted research in person or by phone. When the internet emerged, a few researchers experimented with listserv technology and email interactions, pushing the boundaries of qualitative research. However, the boundaries were hard to push with dial-up connections that were undependable, unavailable, costly, and suspect. A new world of research was being born. Naysayers of online qual questioned the reliability and viability of online qual methods; while some were skeptically cautious, others were more outrightly critical.

Still, in the mid-1990s, some researchers saw the future possibilities and bravely stepped into the unknown by conducting online qualitative research. Jeff Walkowski was one of the small group of pioneers who pursued the possibilities. He began moderating online focus groups using AOL chat rooms, attended some of the first conferences devoted to digital qual, and conducted half-day workshops at IIR (now TMRE) conferences.

In the late 1990s, QRCA established an Online Qualitative Research Task Force co-chaired by Jeff and me. The purpose of the task force was to explore online methodologies and emerging platforms so that members could be informed and educated.

Around this time, Jeff created an online qualitative research course for the RIVA Training Institute. Separately, I created a bulletin board course with Ted Kendall's technology expertise at QualTalk (later Schlesinger's QualBoard and now Sago's QualBoard). Seeing the overlap in our courses and our desire to educate moderators, Jeff and I combined our different courseware and established the Online Moderator Training Institute. OMTI's initial offering was an extensive week-long online course taught using multiple vendor platforms and multiple hands-on experiences with text chats, discussion boards, and video chats with recruited participants.

As researchers and clients discovered that online methods could enable them to reach new respondents, engage with participants in new ways, expand the variety of respondents in a discussion, find busy people, tap into rural areas, and attract younger respondents who know and love technology, online qualitative options were added to more and more researchers' toolboxes.

Which brings us to today. Who knew 30 years ago that qualitative researchers would be:

- embracing online (when appropriate),
- passionate in finding new uses for online qual and creating hybrid methods, and
- happily educating clients who are increasingly knowledgeable and receptive to online qualitative research options?

And who could have known there was a need for an extensive compilation of experienced-based tips? JEFF!

Jeff has poured his breadth of experience and professional heart into this book of highly practical tips. It covers all the when, why, what, which, and how of online qual.

- WHEN and WHY is online the appropriate and preferred methodology?
- WHAT topics and WHICH audiences are particularly suited or not suited for online?
- HOW can we educate clients, select vendors, design an inquiry and moderation strategy, estimate and manage time, and analyze the sometimes-massive amounts of data?

FOREWORD

Before I retired as a researcher, there were a few special books that I repeatedly referred to for information and inspiration. This is one that I would have held near and dear as a new or experienced moderator. It is comprehensive and based on extensive experience. It is an important addition to any researcher's library, and worth its weight in gold!

To all my friends and researchers, use these tips and benefit from the potholes those before you stepped in!

CASEY SWEET
Co-Founder of the Online Moderator Training
Institute, Past QRCA Board Member, Retired

Preface

When I became an independent qualitative research consultant in 1998, my hope was for my work to be split evenly between in-person and online projects. I thoroughly enjoyed both methods, and still do. Furthermore, I truly felt then—as now—that both methods have their place.

Alas, I never achieved the 50–50 split I'd hoped for. I had already established a reputation as one of the experts in the online field, and my project load has consistently been at least 75 percent online. This skew to online work was frustrating because clients seemed to have the misperception that I was an online-only researcher. Over time, however, I eventually embraced this persona. I even considered changing the name of my one-person company from QualCore to Mr. Online. Ultimately, the business name change didn't happen, but this book allows me to finally and publicly claim the title of Mr. Online.

Looking way back to my high school years, my dream was to be a teacher. While I didn't get a teaching degree (long story about why that happened), once I began working in marketing research, I took advantage of every opportunity to share my knowledge with others – delivering presentations at conferences, serving as a guest speaker in college marketing research classes, writing articles, becoming a longstanding trainer for the RIVA Training Institute, co-founding the Online Moderator Training Institute (OMTI), serving a short stint with Research Rockstar, curating a series of webinars for QRCA, and developing the University of Georgia and MRII's online certificate course in qualitative research. "Mr. Online's Playbook" is my latest addition to this series of teaching ventures.

Co-founding the OMTI was something I'm particularly proud of. As part of the marketing effort for OMTI courses, emails were periodically sent out to potential students. Most of those emails included a practical tip about online moderating. The emails went out on Fridays, and because the tips were complimentary to recipients, they were called Freebie Friday emails.

Over the years, the collection of these tips grew. This book is a compilation of those tips amassed over many years. They've been edited, updated, expanded, and organized into what is hopefully a practical guide that will serve new as well as experienced online moderators – now and for years to come. This book is an attempt to codify the best practices that moderators should use through the online qualitative research process. Thank you for reading it.

Acknowledgments

The path to this book was long and sometimes circuitous. There are many who in some way influenced its existence. I would like to thank some of them. They appear here in roughly chronological order.

When I joined M/A/R/C around 1986, I was hired as a quantitative specialist. At that point, I barely knew what qualitative research was. **Gordon Wyner** and **Scott Bailey** were my managers there. They supported my curiosity about qualitative research and authorized the expense for me to get moderator training. In addition, M/A/R/C's relationship with AOL for supplying quantitative research was a catalyst for me to take advantage of AOL chat rooms for my first online focus groups.

When I took the moderator training course from the RIVA Training Institute, I didn't know who **Naomi Henderson** was. Purely by luck, she was one of my two co-trainers in that late 1980s course. It was a firm foundation on which to deepen my basic qualitative research skills, and it was the beginning of a long and fruitful relationship with RIVA.

Very shortly after I joined QRCA, **Casey Sweet** caught wind that I was interested in online qualitative, just as she was. She invited me to join her in a pitch to the QRCA Board of Directors to set up and lead an Online Qualitative Research Task Force. We did that, which exposed me to many of the other early adopters in the online qual field. It was Casey who provided me with that opportunity. Later, we joined forces in the early 2000s to co-found OMTI (Online Moderator Training Institute), which was both a lot of work and even more fun.

Abby Leafe had asked me to moderate a discussion board for her, about weight control among men. Several of her employees observed the session, and pointed out that I was not following a best practice that they had seen their boss (Abby) do. They asked me to please do what Abby does. I was taken aback by this, because I thought I was the expert. Thanks to that experience, I realized that I'm not necessarily the best/perfect moderator, and that there's always room for improvement.

Thomas W. Miller invited me to join him as co-editor of *Qualitative Research Online,* which was published in 2004. I'd like to think that at least some of the material in that book is still useful today. There were many contributors to that book, but I want to give a special shout-out to my QRCA friends who participated in one of two discussion boards that became a focal point of that book: **Pierre Belisle, Lisa Kindig, Hy Mariampolski, Pat Sabena, Casey Sweet, David Van Nuys, Foster Winter,** and **Monica Zinchiak.**

Jennifer Dale and **Susan Abbott** published *Qual-Online: The Essential Guide* in 2015. That book is the only record that I'm aware of about the history and evolution of online qual, and it includes profiles of the people involved in the early days of online qual. I'm so happy that they captured the history. Their book was an inspiration for this one, and I consider *Mr. Online's Playbook* to be the perfect companion to *Qual-Online: The Essential Guide.*

I've known **Mary Beth Solomon** for at least 25 years. She can easily claim to be the godmother of online qual, having moderated online groups before I did. I got to know her through QRCA and when Casey Sweet retired, she has been standing by my side in helping the OMTI continue. Without her help, I'm not sure I could have sustained OMTI on my own.

Last, but not least, I must mention my husband, **Jeff Wyant**. I can be a procrastinator when it comes to big (seemingly insurmountable) projects like putting this book together. But his loveably snarky remarks along the line of, "Yeah sure, the book. You keep saying you need to work on it, but I don't see it. You're never gonna finish that thing." That was just the motivation I needed to keep moving forward—slowly perhaps, but it did get done! (Whew!)

To all of the above, and to many others, I am indebted to you and sincerely thank you.

SECTION ONE

The Fundamentals

The basics that anybody involved with online qualitative research needs to know. Online qual novices should definitely begin here.

• VIDEO | TEXT CHAT | BOARD •

Tip A-1: Be a Champion for ALL Qualitative Methods

Many researchers prefer some qualitative methods over others. For example:

- Some would only consider in-person groups and doubt the value of any text-based online methods.
- Some prefer online methods for lifestyle reasons such as they don't want to leave home if they have young children, or don't want to deal with the hassle of traveling.
- Some feel that real-time text chats are too "surfacy," while appreciating the depth that multi-day discussion boards offer.

While qualitative researchers may have their preferred methods, those preferences should never bias them to steer clients to their preferred methods. Remember that *every* qualitative tool—be it in-person or online—has its place. Acknowledge that no single method is categorically better than the other. Each has its advantages and disadvantages, and each might work well in some situations and not as well in others.

This means that all researchers owe it to their clients (whether internal or external) to be familiar with *all* available methods both in-person and online, 2) understand the fundamental pros and cons of each, and 3) recognize and advocate for the best research methods, not just those they personally prefer.

1

• VIDEO | TEXT CHAT | BOARD •

Tip A-2: Don't Fear Online Qual

Are you new to online qualitative and do you have some jitters about it? If so, relax. Learning to moderate online is like learning any new skill, be it riding a bike, performing in front of an audience, or learning a new language. Commit to it and those initial fears will likely melt away fairly quickly.

Here are some tips to help ease your entry into moderating online focus groups:

- **Talk to your clients.** If you don't suggest online qualitative options, your clients may not either. Position online qual as an opportunity for both of you to explore together. Let your clients be your ally as you delve into online qual.

- **Offer to do a pro bono project.** Not finding allies within your network of business professionals? Non-profits crave information to help with decision-making. They will most likely need to incur some costs, but if you offer your time for free, it becomes a win-win for both you and the non-profit.

- **Start with options that feel comfortable.** Assuming that all online methods (video chats, real-time text chats, and asynchronous discussion boards) would meet the information objectives of a particular project, shy away from those methods that make you nervous in any way. If the relatively laid-back pace of a discussion board appeals to you, then look for projects that lend themselves to that method. If you'd like something more like traditional in-person focus groups, then search out potential projects that would be well-suited to online video chats.

- **Go easy on yourself.** While an experienced online moderator might be willing to handle multiple text or video chats in a day, that's probably too much for a beginner. Take it easy. Give yourself time to learn from each session.

1 | THE FUNDAMENTALS

- **Take advantage of platform providers.** They want to earn your continued business, so they will do everything they can to help you succeed in your first foray into online qual. Ask them, "What can you do to make this easier for me?"

- **Practice with friends and family.** Platform providers will typically let beginners use their platform for free for practice sessions especially those that you don't profit from.

- **Get training.** The Online Moderator Training Institute offers individual and group training for all skill levels (www.OnlineModerator.com). Full disclosure: I am the co-founder of the OMTI.

- **Partner with an expert.** If formal training is not an option, find someone who might be able to coach you through your first project. QRCA's Find a Researcher feature (www.qrca.org) can help you locate an online moderator. The Online Moderator Training Institute offers coaching as well.

- **Co-moderate.** Find someone (perhaps in your own organization) who also wants to learn to moderate online. Support, coach, and learn from each other. Sharing the "burden" of learning a new skill will make the task easier. (See Tip G-10 for info on co-moderating text chats.)

As you can see, there are many ways to get started. Pick one or more from the list above and go for it!

• VIDEO •

Tip A-3: Think of Video Chats as the "Kiddie Pool" for New Online Moderators

Trying something new always comes with risks. If you've not done any qualitative work online, it might feel a bit scary to try it for the first time.

For beginners, however—especially those who are more risk averse—video chat is the perfect method to help you quickly climb the online qual learning curve. Just as children typically learn to swim by being led into a wading pool, video chat may be the gentlest way to learn to moderate online.

Video chats are perfect for beginners because they are most like traditional focus groups.

- We see all participants
- We hear all participants
- The discussion guide looks the same
- Each person talks one at a time
- Session length is typically 90–120 minutes
- Many activities that are used in face-to-face groups can be replicated in video chats

Because of all these similarities to in-person groups, the anxiety level is considerably lower than with any of the other methods e.g., real-time text chats and multi-day discussion boards, making it a good option to start with.

Video chat platforms can be used for IDIs (in-depth interviews) as well as groups. If you're nervous about groups, consider a "pre-test" or a "dry run" with just one or two participants. You can increase the number of participants in your groups as you grow more comfortable with the technique.

If it's your clients who are reticent about trying online qualitative, you can gently guide them into the online qual pool by recommending video chats. They will be surprised at how similar a video chat is compared with in-person interviews or discussions.

• VIDEO | TEXT CHAT | BOARD •

TIP A-4: Watch Your Language

It is unfortunate that there are ambiguous and confusing terms used in reference to online qualitative research—not just by those new to the field but by experienced practitioners as well. Hopefully in time a consensus will build and there will be a universal set of terms that everyone understands.

Synchronous vs. asynchronous. These are the only terms about which there seems to be no confusion.

Synchronous online methods are those in which all participants are

1 | THE FUNDAMENTALS

present at the same time and for a set period of time (relatively short, usually two hours or less)—just like in an in-person focus group. Synchronous methods include text chats and video chats (see definitions below).

Asynchronous online methods are those in which participants are NOT likely to be present at the same time, and the discussion platform remains open for an extended period of time—typically multiple days.

Online Focus Groups. To some, *online focus group* is a generic term that covers all forms of online qualitative. Others use this term only when referring to real-time sessions—NOT multi-day discussion boards. Furthermore, some think of video chats as the only form of online focus group. *In this book, we consider all online qualitative methods to be online focus groups.* Each method has its own name:

- **Text Chats.** In this book, the term *text chat* is used to describe a synchronous method in which data collection uses text only. Voice and video are not used. Text chats may also be referred to as real-time text groups or real-time online focus groups.

- **Video Chats.** This is the visual and audio version of an online synchronous chat. Video chats are the online method that is most similar to in-person focus groups. Video chats are sometimes called webcam focus groups or webcam chats. **For consistency, we use the term** *video chat* **in this book.**

- **Discussion Boards.** In this book we use the term *discussion board* to refer to any asynchronous online method. Discussion boards are sometimes referred to as bulletin boards, asynchronous focus groups, and online community boards.

If somebody asks, "What would it cost to run a couple of online focus groups?" click the pause button and find out exactly what they mean, because costs differ for each type of online session. Take the opportunity to educate the inquirer about the three forms of online qualitative, how they differ, and the pros and cons of each.

Communities. Those who specialize in creating and managing online communities are typically talking about large groups of participants—

dozens, if not hundreds or even thousands—who are engaged in ongoing research for an organization, research company, or a client-side brand over an extended period of time, weeks, months, and perhaps even years. Members of these communities are often asked to participate in quantitative as well as qualitative projects, and one or more of the online qualitative methods described above may be used over the course of time. In rare cases, if there are enough community members in a particular market, they may occasionally meet in person.

One could argue that regardless of the number of participants or which online method is used, the moderator's job is always to foster a sense of community in any online focus group. Furthermore, one could argue that smaller, short-term projects have the potential for fostering a stronger sense of community than larger, longer-term projects. For that reason, reserving the term *online community* for extended research involvements may be considered a disservice to the sense of community that can emerge in smaller, shorter-term methods. That said, **to be more consistent with current vernacular, in this book we reserve the term online community for longer-term projects with many participants.**

Thus, keep these terms in mind when discussing online qualitative options with your clients. And if anyone approaches you and uses the above terms, it would be wise to avoid any misunderstandings by confirming what those terms mean.

• VIDEO | TEXT CHAT | BOARD •

Tip A-5: Recognize that Moderating Online is Different than Moderating In-Person

When I dipped my toes into the online qualitative pool in the mid-1990s, I thought, "It can't be that difficult. I'm already a good focus group moderator with a successful practice. Moderating online will be the same as moderating in-person: establish rapport, ask questions, and probe as necessary. Easy!"

It was an eye-opener to realize that moderating online is NOT the same as moderating in-person. Online moderating requires every skill

1 | THE FUNDAMENTALS   7

we already use for in-person focus groups *PLUS* additional skills. Here are some examples of the extra skills needed in text-based methods—text chats and discussion boards:

- **Adapting guides.** For any text-based group, more time needs to be spent on the discussion guide. Care needs to be taken to make them more precise.

- **Being human.** Participants can't see or hear us, so online moderators need to know how to form a "virtual" bond with them so that they are fully engaged.

- **Setting the pace.** Without being able to see and hear participants in real-time text chats, online moderators need to develop a sense of when it's time to ask the next question. We do not want to rush the group, nor do we want to let it go too slowly.

- **Shaping participant behavior.** Discussion board participants sometimes fail to answer questions fully or clearly. The online moderator needs to train participants to always provide complete and unambiguous responses.

- **Managing expectations.** Online groups tend to be new experiences for both participants and observers. It's typically the online moderator who's counted on to coach on what to expect and how to be most productive.

While video chats are most similar to moderating in-person, there remain differences that a novice video-chat moderator may not consider. Some examples are:

- **Exercising crowd control.** People talking over one another is much more disruptive in video chats than in-person. Online moderators need to know how to manage this gracefully.

- **Overcoming limited visual cues.** Yes, we can see participants in video chats, but we typically see little more than head shots. We seldom see their hands, and maybe see just a bit of posture. Online moderators need to build skills to compensate for this.

Researchers take a risk when they jump into online moderation without guidance and practice. Disappoint a client because of mistakes in your first online groups, and chances are low that you will be called back for more work.

• TEXT CHAT | BOARD •

TIP A-6: Know when One Text-Based Method Should Be Used Over Another

There are two text-based online qualitative research methods: real- time chats—short, usually 90 minutes in length—and discussion boards that typically last days. Those who are new to online methods are often confused about when one of these methods should be recommended over the other.

In many instances, valid arguments can be made to use either real-time chats or discussion boards. At that point, it sometimes comes down to a budget and timing decision that steers one to chats, which are faster and cheaper, or boards.

There are times, however, when a clear recommendation can be made for one method versus another. One way to help decide which method to recommend is to assess whether we want quick, gut-level reactions to the questions and issues we raise, or if we want participants to be more thoughtful about their answers. Another way of looking at it is to decide how deep we want to go in terms of participant responses.

Chats. With real-time text chats, the name of the game is speed. Moderators want to keep everyone at the same pace, so the questions asked are typically designed to yield responses that may be only a sentence or two in length. In chats, respondents don't want to be left behind, so they tend to type quickly, and in short bursts of text. Thus, the real-time chat environment promotes quick-thinking and doesn't provide much of an opportunity for participants to "over-think" their responses. Real-time chats are perfect for things like:

- Ad/copy testing.
- Early-stage "simple" concept evaluation—identifying which of many concepts should be developed more fully.

1 | THE FUNDAMENTALS

- Capturing consumer language.
- Developing response lists for a quantitative survey.

Boards. Discussion boards, on the other hand, give participants the luxury of thinking through an answer before posting. In fact, participants might compose a response and spend a lot of time editing it before posting. Some might ponder the question for minutes or hours before putting their fingers to the keyboard. Moderators in a discussion board don't need to worry about keeping everyone in sync with each other, so they are more likely to ask questions that require essay-length answers. Thus, discussion boards are the more appropriate choice in these instances:

- Evaluating "complex" concepts such as those that take a long time to read and digest.
- Respondent story-telling—in-depth summaries of product or service experiences.
- When activities will be required such as visiting websites, taking photos, or reporting on a shopping trip.
- When we anticipate that many questions will require long responses —paragraphs rather than a phrase or sentence.

· BOARD ·

TIP A-7: Realize that Moderating Discussion Boards Takes a Lot of Time

Because asynchronous discussion boards are unlike any synchronous (real-time) online or in-person focus group, those who are new to moderating discussion boards often ask, "How much time does it take to moderate discussion boards?"

A good rule-of-thumb is to expect to spend about 4 hours each day moderating a typical discussion board. This rule-of-thumb is based on the following assumptions:

- There are 12–16 active participants.
- Each participant spends 30–45 minutes per day on the board.
- Participants are able to see others' posts and interact with each other.

- The moderator *actively* moderates (i.e., does not put the discussion board on "auto-pilot."). This includes reading all posts as they come in, probing as needed to elicit complete answers and clarify ambiguities, and encouraging interaction among participants.

Changes in these assumptions will impact the amount of time needed to moderate. Here are some examples:

- If there are only 20–30 minutes of activities per participant per day, less moderator time will be required.
- With 20+ participants, there's more to read, which will naturally increase moderator time.
- If the board is used for one-on-one interviews, then needing to repeat probes and losing the efficiency of participants building on each other's posts will require more time of the moderator. (See Tip B-9 for more on this.)

This rule-of-thumb of 4 hours per day of moderating a board is valuable, because work schedules can be more effectively managed and pricing is more accurate at the beginning, sparing any surprising "price adjustments" at the end of the project.

Some moderators are faster readers than others, and in some ways more efficient than others. Thus, use this rule of thumb as an initial guide and adjust accordingly. And don't forget to budget time for project management each day—sending daily reminders, nudging inactive participants, leading daily debrief sessions with the client team, etc.

• VIDEO | TEXT CHAT •

Tip A-8: Understand the Pros and Cons of Text Chats vs. Video Chats

There are two options for real-time (synchronous) online qualitative sessions: text chats and video chats. They both have their advantages. It's good to keep these in mind when deciding which method to recommend in a given set of circumstances. Here, we are comparing text chat platforms to video chat platforms *that have been customized for qualitative research.*

1 | THE FUNDAMENTALS

Advantages of Real-Time Text Chats

- **Anonymity is maximized.** If a study will benefit from participants being anonymous, text is better than video. By not being able to see or hear participants, and by giving them an alias or pseudonym, text chats preserve anonymity. Participant anonymity is especially useful in employee research, research on sensitive subjects, and when participants may know one another—neighbors, peers in competing organizations, for example.

- **Potentially more data.** In text chats, participants can all "talk" at the same time without interrupting anyone. This allows everyone to answer every question.

- **May be less expensive.** Platform usage fees are typically less for text chats than for video chat platforms designed for qualitative research. Note that general-purpose video chat platforms like Zoom are less expensive than customized video chat platforms. Also, transcripts are an automatic byproduct of text chats, making them free, and transcripts from text chats will be 100 percent accurate, unlike machine-generated transcripts generated from the platform.

Advantages of Video Chats

- **"Closer" to participants.** With video chats, we see and hear our respondents. We capture voice inflection and body language. If we need to watch them do something, or if we need participants to show us something, video chats make that easy.

- **More "natural" conversation.** While we're all accustomed to typing emails and texts, talking is still faster and easier for all involved. Participants are more likely to "think out loud" in a video chat, and sometimes it's useful to observe participants going through that process.

- **Video clips are easy to include in reports.** It's relatively easy to extract clips to include in reports. And those clips can be valuable in driving home important findings and recommendations.

- **Availability of breakout rooms.** If it's important to break the group into two or more smaller groups at some point, some video chat platforms have this capability.

• VIDEO •

Tip A-9: Know What General-Purpose Video Chat Platforms Offer (and Don't Offer)

There are two types of video chat platforms: general-purpose ones and those that are designed specifically for qualitative research. Many of the general-purpose platforms (e.g., Zoom, Skype, WebEx, GoToMeeting, and Teams) offer basic functionality for free, and versions with enhanced features for a fee. Platforms that are customized for qualitative research will cost more.

It's tempting to forego the customized platforms to keep research costs as low as they can be. However, before choosing a relatively inexpensive general-purpose platform, it's important to understand what they include, and what you may be missing. Here is a short list of the drawbacks of general-purpose platforms:

- **No waiting rooms.** Some general-purpose platforms may have what they call a waiting room, but those in the waiting room can't converse with each other, and the moderator cannot drop in and chat with those who are there. There is no graceful way to collect additional info to help decide who to keep and who to let go when more recruits show up than were expected, and there is no polite way to excuse those who the team decides to not admit into the discussion when too many people show up.

- **No tech support.** General-purpose platforms are DIY (do-it-yourself) platforms. If any technical issues come up, you are on your own. If your participants or observers run into tech issues, they will rely on you or your own support staff to offer help.

- **No observation rooms.** General-purpose video chat platforms do not distinguish between participants and observers. We trust observers to keep their webcams and microphones off. There is a way for users to "not show" the observers on their screen (those who do not turn their video on), but not all know how to use it; in that case, each observer still shows on the participants' screens, serving as a constant reminder that others are watching and listening.

1 | THE FUNDAMENTALS

- **No in-app communication tools.** While chat functionality is available in general-purpose platforms, it is for one-on-one communication—NOT one-to-many—moderator to all observers—conversation. Thus, a separate app may be required to hold those conversations.
- **Limited activities.** General-purpose platforms tend to offer polling functionality, and they may offer whiteboard capabilities as well to show concepts, or to use as a digital easel, but other capabilities found in customized platforms will not be available.
- **Limited recording capabilities.** Most general-purpose video chat platforms have recording capability, but if break-out rooms are part of the platform, recordings of those breakout rooms may or may not be available.

It should be noted that some companies have taken a platform like Zoom and added capabilities to it to provide more versatility to the research community. Thus, in addition to general-purpose platforms and customized-for-research platforms, there is a new group of suppliers that are a blend of both.

Considering all of the above, general-purpose platforms should be considered only when at least one of the following conditions is met:

- Budget is extremely tight.
- Separate waiting room is not required.
- Separate observer room is not required.
- No special features beyond polling and an available whiteboard are required.
- There will be few (if any) observers.
- Easy communication between the moderator and the observer group is not required.

Technology is rapidly changing, and it is likely that the general-purpose video chat platforms will continue to offer enhancements that put them more on par with customized video chat platforms. As such, it's up to the researcher to know what they need and match it to what's available. And in the meantime, researchers should at least consider using the video chat platforms that have been designed specifically for qualitative research.

· BOARD ·

Tip A-10: Know the Differences Among Discussion Board Platforms

Choosing an online discussion board platform is like choosing a new vehicle. All vehicles do the same thing—get you from Point A to Point B. But they are different in many ways; price, reliability, accessories, reputation, gas mileage, etc. It's the same with online discussion board platforms; they all provide a means of collecting data digitally over an extended period of time, but they accomplish it in different ways.

- **Appearance.** Each will have a different look and feel. This could affect which would be better for research: kids vs. adults, B2B vs. B2C, etc.

- **Features.** The built-in optional features that are available (e.g., polls, uploading photos or videos, picture sorts, collage tools, etc.) will vary. Some offer more than others. Some offer different sets of tools. The tools one would like to use for a given project could impact platform choice.

- **Thread Layout.** Some do a better job of helping users visually see the flow of an interactive group discussion. This is unimportant when the discussion board is being used for in-depth interviews, because it's very easy to see the back-and-forth between moderator and participant. (See also Tip C-11.)

- **Level of Service.** Some are full-service while others are not. Full-service can include things like 24/7 tech support, access to online panels, recruitment, payment of incentives, and uploading discussion guides. For online research novices and first-time users of a platform, these services may be very important, while they may not be as important to more seasoned online researchers.

Existing discussion board platform providers make changes to their platforms, some more frequently than others. On top of that, new platform providers occasionally enter the market. Online moderators who want to provide the best platform under any given set of circumstances should stay abreast of the changes that take place in the online qualitative research platform business. (See Tip A-16 about ways to stay informed about developments in the platform provider landscape.)

• BOARD •

TIP A-11: Exercise Caution When Using DIY Discussion Board Platforms

As the online discussion board industry has evolved, stripped-down versions of discussion board platforms have become available. These may be called DIY platforms because they are strictly do-it-yourself, with typically only basic capabilities and little (if any) technical support. They may also be called limited-service platforms. When platform needs are simple, DIY platforms are attractive because using them can help reduce project costs.

Newer online moderators, however, should approach DIY platforms with great care. Full-service discussion board platforms typically come with live tech support that's available nearly 24/7. Readily-available tech support offers several key benefits which should be considered—especially for newer discussion board moderators:

Safety Net for Moderator. For newer online moderators, it's good to have Tech Support readily available to answer questions about how to accomplish something, or to address any system issues that may arise. In essence, tech support offers a "safety net" to newer moderators who are likely to be a bit more anxious about using newer technology. Tech support allows the moderator to concentrate on moderating and not worry about technical issues.

Safety Net for Participants and Observers. Tech Support is also useful for participants and observers who run into issues, such as login issues, uncertainty about how to do certain things on the discussion board, etc. Without tech support, they will reach out to the moderator for assistance. This can be nerve-wracking, especially for a newbie whose main focus is on moderation—NOT on providing tech support.

As might be expected, limited-service platforms will likely not have all of the "bells and whistles" found in full-service platforms. Newer online moderators might not know which features are "standard" on all platforms, and which ones are only available on the more expensive full-service platforms. Thus, newbie online moderators should think carefully about which features they'd like to have available, and double-check about the availability of those features on any DIY platforms (and full-service platforms, as well) under consideration.

My advice for newer online moderators is to "play it safe" by using full-service platforms in the earlier stages of their online moderating career. Once they gain sufficient experience, they can more confidently explore the use of DIY platforms.

• VIDEO | TEXT CHAT | BOARD •

Tip A-12: Be Familiar with Which Tools Are Available on Which Platforms

Most online qualitative platform providers offer optional apps that can both engage participants and hopefully lead to deeper insights. Here is a small sample of the types of tools that are generally considered most useful.

- **Polls.** Polls are fairly standard in all platforms. Polls are great for capturing quick reactions, and then using the poll results as a starting point for further discussion.

- **Sorting/Ranking.** Some platform providers offer an app which allows the moderator to present a set of things (e.g., brand names, short descriptions of concepts). Participants are able to drag and drop each item into a particular order or sort into groups (e.g., brands aware of but never used, brands ever used, brands no longer used).

- **Mark-Up.** For in-person groups, we sometimes want to capture independent initial feedback on concepts before having an open discussion about it. We'll hand a copy to each participant and ask them to mark up the page to show what they like or dislike, and flag parts they have questions about. Some online platform providers offer an app which allows participants to complete this task digitally.

1 | THE FUNDAMENTALS

- **Collages.** Having participants collect images to arrange on a page, then having them share the collage with the group and tell the story of what the collage means is a great exercise with many benefits. Some online platforms provide digital tools to accomplish the same thing—typically having the participant use a predetermined assortment of images.
- **Sharing Photos, Videos.** As mentioned in other Tips, photos and videos can be a great value-add in qualitative reports. Many platform providers make it easy for participants to upload photos and record videos for analysis and inclusion in reports.

The specific tools offered vary from one platform provider to another. It's good for researchers to check platform provider websites or communicate with representatives to keep up with which apps they may have available. If you have a particular activity you'd like to use but don't see it available, consider contacting one or more platform providers and asking if they might be able to develop the app for you; they can market the tool for others and potentially offer an app that no other platform provider offers.

• VIDEO | TEXT CHAT | BOARD •

Tip A-13: Know that Sampling Options are Increasing

Once upon a time, there was no such thing as online panel providers. In the "olden days" of online qualitative, we hand-picked a widely scattered group of focus group facilities across the country to get a mix of people to participate in online focus groups. It was cumbersome coordinating the efforts of several independent focus group facilities but it worked.

Then online panel companies appeared, and they grew. Most of their panelists participate in online quantitative surveys, but those panels were open to recruiting for online qualitative projects as well. Over time, we became less dependent on the brick-and-mortar focus group facilities for recruitment.

But then focus group facilities began to merge, and in the process they developed their own regional and national panels, and made their recruitment services available not just for in-person projects, but online projects as well. Now, many brick-and-mortar focus group facilities compete with the online panel companies for online qualitative recruitment projects. This is especially helpful in instances when we want to recruit from a particularly small geography. While an online panel may not have enough sample in a narrowly-defined geography to fill an online focus group, in-person facilities in those geographies are well-positioned to supplement the recruitment efforts of a panel company or they may be willing to take on the entire recruitment effort.

Thus, if you're looking for a general nationwide representation in your online focus groups, you might choose to work with an online panel company. However, depending on how narrowly focused your desired geography is, you may be better served by working with brick-and-mortar facilities at or near those geographies.

• VIDEO | TEXT CHAT | BOARD •

Tip A-14: Remember that Sensitive Subjects Work Well Online

All online qualitative methods (video chats, real-time text chats, and multi-day discussion boards) are naturally less intimate than in-person qualitative projects. Some say that because of this lesser intimacy, it may be unproductive to discuss sensitive topics in an online setting.

Based on many past experiences, it is abundantly clear to me that difficult topics can be effectively discussed online. Tears have been shed during video chats, anger and frustration came through loud and clear in a discussion board among one organization's employees regarding work conditions, and I've seen an outpouring of compassion and support among participants in text chats. There's no doubt that we ARE able to get below the surface and explore deep-seated emotions even in online qualitative.

How is this possible? This seems to stem from three things:

- **Comfort zone.** With online studies, participants are usually in their home, not in a sterile focus group facility. They are in their comfort zone, which makes it easier for them to open up to moderators and to other participants.

1 | THE FUNDAMENTALS

- **Anonymity.** Not being in the physical presence of others gives participants permission to share their emotions without embarrassment.
- **Mutual support.** If it's a group discussion, knowing that other participants share the same issue or experiences provides a level of camaraderie they seldom experience in their daily lives. Being in a group with others who share their concerns can be cathartic—even online.

To make sure these sessions go well, online researchers need to:

- **Screen carefully.** Be sure that those recruited fit the criteria, let participants know why they were selected, and in group discussions explain what they will have in common with their fellow participants.
- **Be open and welcoming.** Make participants comfortable and make it easy for them to participate—before and during the data collection process.
- **Ask good questions.** Engage and intrigue participants. Include questions and activities that add an element of surprise to the discussion.
- **Provide a safe haven.** Make sure that nobody is hurt in any way by the discussion. If a participant is uncomfortable answering certain questions, honor that reluctance and move on.
- **Listen intently.** Demonstrate understanding of what participants tell us. Leave no doubt that they are providing the information needed, and assure them that we sincerely appreciate their input.
- **Probe empathetically.** As appropriate, take participants down a road of discussion that reveals more than just surface-level perceptions, opinions, beliefs, and attitudes.

Online qualitative methods are not a barrier to digging below the surface and exploring sensitive subjects. On the contrary, the online environment has the potential to enable participants to share at least as much as might be shared during in-person focus groups.

• VIDEO | TEXT CHAT | BOARD •

Tip A-15: Consider How Increased Reliance on Mobile Devices Impacts Online Qual

According to statista.com, among U.S. households . . .

- 85% owned a smartphone in 2021 (up from 68% in 2015)
- 74% owned a laptop or desktop in 2019 (down from a high of 78%)
- 53% owned a tablet in 2021 (steady for about four years)

In the U.S. and other parts of the world, there is decreasing dependence on laptops and desktops for internet access and more reliance on mobile devices. This has implications for online qualitative— *especially for **group** discussions*. As pointed out in Tip D-4, this is because the user experience during online group discussions is optimized using larger-format devices (laptops and desktops).

Thus, when conducting any online group discussion:

- Include a question on the screener to be sure participants have a laptop or desktop.
- When a session begins, remind participants that they should be using a laptop or desktop.

In qualitative research, we don't claim to have fully representative samples in our study. Still, we do our best to assure that the full range of people in the target market gets represented in our studies. This becomes increasingly difficult, however, when we know that a substantial percentage of the target population cannot participate in online group discussions because they don't have an appropriate device with which to participate.

If there are concerns that too many in your target group won't have access to a laptop or desktop, or if too many are dropping out of the screening process because they only have a smartphone or tablet, consider these options:

- Shift the design from online group discussions to one-on-one online interviews. In that case, smartphones will work perfectly.

1 | THE FUNDAMENTALS

- Use a mixed-method approach. For example, conduct online focus groups among those with a laptop or desktop, and online IDIs with those with only a smartphone.

Remember that as consumers use fewer large-screen devices and more small/mobile devices, research designs may need to be adapted to compensate for these changes.

• VIDEO | TEXT CHAT | BOARD •

Tip A-16: Keep Up with Latest Developments in Online Qualitative Platforms

It's not easy keeping up with all of the changes in the online focus group platform industry. New platforms emerge, some make significant improvements and change names, and some fade away.

Once you find platforms that you like and are comfortable with, you will likely stick with them and not feel the need to investigate others. On the other hand, you may want to keep tabs on what's new. If you are a newbie to online qual, you're probably starting from scratch and would like as much information as possible. A list of platform providers could be provided here, but it will likely be out of date within six months.

Besides web searches for online focus group platforms, what other options are available to keep up with this industry? Here are some suggestions:

- **Subscribe to Quirk's.** If you're in the marketing research industry, it's free to subscribe. Quirk's is a print magazine and a comprehensive website. Quirk's has lots of advertisers, so that's one way to become aware of new online qual platform providers.
- **Attend market research conferences.** Whether those conferences are in-person or virtual, there are likely to be online qual platform providers with exhibits.
- **Join QRCA.** QRCA members have access to a members-only Forum, where you can post a query about the latest platforms that other members may have used or investigated.

- **Join Relevant Social Media Groups.** There is a "Qual Group from QRCA" on Facebook and LinkedIn. These are closed groups to which you need to be admitted, but if you work in (or are interested in working in) the qualitative field, chances are very high that you will be admitted.

It takes work to keep up with what's going on with the online focus group platform landscape, but it's worth it.

• TEXT CHAT | BOARD •

Tip A-17: Be Prepared for Investment Requirements in Community Panel Management

Long-term communities may last for weeks, months, and perhaps even years. The number of members in a community can range from a few dozen (in very low incidence categories) to literally thousands. At the launch of a community, participants are recruited in hopes that all will be longstanding community members—ideally for the lifetime of the community. However, there is bound to be churn; those who become inactive or ask to leave will need to be replaced. Also, depending on changes in their demographics and product or service usage, some members may need to be weeded out of the community—for example: from a community of new moms, those whose children are well past a certain age.

The marketing adage about keeping customers applies to community members as well: it's a lot less costly to keep a current member than to find and onboard a new one. Do NOT take community panel management lightly, otherwise an online moderator might find him- or herself with a dwindling pool of respondents that might be skewed or biased in some way.

It's best for community members to be assigned activities on a regular basis. Of course, the information needs of the community owner will ebb and flow, with periods of heavy activity followed by relatively quiet periods. However, lulls can give the impression that the community is no longer needed; this is when there is a high risk of members losing interest and leaving. Agree to a schedule of activities (e.g., twice a week, every other week or so) and stick to it as much as possible. An important part of community panel management is giving the impression that the community is "always on."

Do not take community management lightly. One could make a career out of community management. A simple online search for "online community management" will instantly reveal a wealth of resources. Use them.

SECTION 2

Selling Online Qualitative

Tips on what to say to clients (internal or external) to convince them to at least consider online qualitative options.

• VIDEO | TEXT CHAT | BOARD •

Tip B-1: Tout the Ever-Increasing Pool of Online Consumers

Because internet access is so pervasive in most developed countries, and increasingly more in less-developed countries, too, one could argue that the sample pool from which to recruit participants is better, larger and more diverse than the sample pool for in-person focus groups. It's worth pointing out to clients how we can benefit from this larger pool. Here are some examples:

- **No geographic limitations.** We are not limited to those who live relatively close to focus group facilities in major markets; we can include those who live in exurbs and even rural locations.

- **More inclusive.** We can include those with a physical disability that makes it difficult for them to leave their home and visit a focus group facility. Also, we have access to people who would like to share their opinions but are unwilling to travel to a focus group facility to share those opinions.

- **Fewer "professional respondents."** While many consumers belong to online panels, most of what they participate in are quantitative surveys. In our experience, most participants in online qualitative projects are doing so for the first time. It is a novel experience for them. Thus, we're less likely to encounter "professional respondents" (something that most researchers want to avoid) in online qualitative.

Even though we never claim that qualitative research is based on truly representative samples (that's a claim of quantitative research), we actually have a better chance of tapping into a more diverse and representative set of participants when we focus on online projects instead of in-person ones.

• VIDEO | TEXT CHAT | BOARD •

Tip B-2: Highlight More Authentic Participant Feedback

Do you need to make the strongest case possible to "sell in" the idea of online qualitative? If so, be sure to point out that participants in online qual may be more authentic than those during in-person interview settings. How might they be more authentic?

- **More comfortable.** Participants don't have to go to a focus group facility. They can participate from anywhere with internet access; most choose the comfort of their own homes. Being "on their own turf" puts them more at ease and makes them more open with us as they talk.

- **Anonymity promotes openness.** Especially with text-based online qual options—where participants cannot see or hear each other— all are on equal footing. Each participant's voice is as strong as the other. Being anonymous breaks down barriers to expressing how they really feel.

- **Less inhibited.** Being physically removed from other participants reduces their inhibitions. They don't need to look other participants in the eye. They don't have to walk beside them to the parking lot after an in-person group. They are less likely to worry about offending someone if they happen to disagree with them. They are more likely to say exactly what's on their mind.

- **Fewer professional respondents.** Because online qual is still relatively new, the number of "professional respondents" in online qual projects is small. So, for most online qual participants, it's a new experience, and they are less likely to be jaded participants.

- **More diverse pool of potential recruits.** As pointed out in Tip B-1, we have an opportunity with online qual to tap into the opinions and attitudes of those who would never consider attending an in-person focus group or IDI, as well as those who are too far away from a focus group facility to be considered for recruitment. This gives us a wider pool of participants to recruit from.

Online qual isn't the best approach all of the time, but there are some very good reasons to consider it. When offering online qual, don't forget to point out a clear advantage of online qual—the opportunity to un-cover more authentic responses.

• VIDEO | TEXT CHAT | BOARD •

TIP B-3: Propose Side-by-Side Designs for Online Qualitative Skeptics

Before the COVID pandemic, there were many qualitative research buy-ers who had steered clear of any form of online qualitative. COVID forced buyers to make use of online methods (mostly video chats) to help guide their decision-making processes.

There may be less resistance to video chats than pre-COVID, but even among qualitative practitioners there is a longing for the "good old days" of in-person research. Text-based online methods are still kept at bay by some buyers, because they are not considered to be "tried-and-true." These buyers and practitioners want "proof" of the efficacy of online methods before they'll consider trying them.

Unfortunately, there's little to no "proof" in the literature about the ef-ficacy of online vs. offline (in-person) groups. Those of us who do a lot of online work can share anecdotes about the power of online qualitative, but research results are almost always proprietary, so the documented "proof" that skeptical buyers are looking for is hard to come by.

One way around this is to propose a research design that incorpo-rates BOTH online and offline methods. When we have done this in the past, we propose doing the in-person groups first, followed by an online group or two. This dual-method approach serves multiple purposes:

- **Familiar.** It makes buyers comfortable that a methodology they have faith in (in-person) is an integral part of the design.
- **Lower Perceived Risk.** It minimizes their sense of "risk" in the very unlikely circumstance that the online sessions go awry.

2 | SELLING ONLINE QUALITATIVE   27

- **Apples to Apples Comparison.** It gives them (and you, the researcher) a rare opportunity to do some side-by-side research on results from the two methods. "Do we reach the same conclusions with both methods?" Of course, there may be some subtle differences between the online and offline results, but no more than the differences we typically witness as we go from one in-person group to another.

- **Maximizes Potential Success of Online.** By doing the in-person groups first, we learn what works and doesn't work in the guide, allowing us to tweak the online guide and maximize the success of the online group.

The upshot of this is that you become a hero for successfully getting your client to try out something new, and they become heroes in their organization for introducing new qualitative research methods. It's a win-win for everybody.

• TEXT CHAT | BOARD •

TIP B-4: Schedule a Demo for Prospective Clients

The COVID-19 pandemic forced many users of focus groups to pivot to online focus groups for the first time. Most likely, they were introduced to video chats and are now well-versed in them. In that case, offering a demo of a video chat is probably not needed. However, don't rule out a demo for decision-makers who've never done any focus groups and expect them to be done in-person.

This tip focuses more on text-based online focus group options— real-time text chats and discussion boards. There are many who have doubts about the utility of those methods. They may be reluctant to "take a risk" on what, to them, is an "unproven" technique.

Demo Real-Time Text Chat. If you offer to run a short demonstration of a real-time text chat, they will appreciate the offer and will likely take advantage of it. A 15–20 minute chat on a general topic (like pets, vacations, movies, or snacking) should suffice. You might assign the observer role to one or more members of the client team, and the participant role to up to six others. If your client team isn't large enough to fill these roles, ask the platform provider to provide staff to stand-in as participants to make the demo more realistic. An additional 10–15 minute debrief after the demonstration should resolve any other questions or concerns they may have.

Demo Online Discussion Board. The same thing can be done with discussion boards. In this case, you might consider giving each member of the client team both roles (Participant and Observer). In the Participant role, allow them to introduce themselves and answer 3–5 questions on a general topic of your choosing. Post all of the questions at once, leave the board open for 2–3 days, actively moderate the discussion to encourage interaction, and schedule a 15–30 minute debrief session to collect their feedback and answer any questions they may have.

Platform providers are typically open to providing free use of their platforms for demonstration purposes. This means that there's no out-of-pocket expense to you. You only need to spend some time up-front getting the demo set-up, and also making time for a post-demo debrief.

Giving the client team an opportunity to "test drive" the platform is likely to reduce their resistance to using a new (for them) qualitative research tool.

• VIDEO | TEXT CHAT | BOARD •

Tip B-5: Self-Fund a Project for Future Demo Purposes

Research buyers tend to be risk-averse and reluctant to invest in a method that they've not had a chance to grow comfortable with on their own. Post-COVID, this is less likely to be the case with video chats, but some researchers remain reluctant to take a chance on text-based online methods.

It would be great to show examples of past online projects, but most are proprietary and cannot be shared. Running a demo with clients as participants is another option, but it's often difficult to line up enough client-side participants for a realistic demo.

Another option is to invest in a demo project to be shared with multiple prospective clients. It will involve time and expense on your part, but

2 | SELLING ONLINE QUALITATIVE   29

remember that this is an investment, and there are ways to minimize the out-of-pocket expenses. Here's how to build your demo project:

1. **Choose a platform provider.** Ask if they will give you a price break for business development purposes. As long as you are not profiting directly from the session, they may be willing to provide free access; after all, it showcases their platform.

2. **Recruit friends as participants.** Minimize recruitment costs by relying on your personal network. If the platform provider has a relationship with an online panel provider, perhaps they can help you get a deep discount for finding participants.

3. **Keep the demo short.** Demos do not need to be long. A 30–45 minute text or video chat session should be sufficient. For discussion boards, running them for a day, or two at most, will be sufficient.

4. **Offer a small incentive.** If you keep the session short and have an interesting topic, friends don't need a high incentive. Consider offering a $10–$20 gift card.

5. **Choose a general topic.** This will help with recruitment and make it easier for clients in different industries to relate to. If you are marketing to a particular industry, you may want to tailor your topic to that industry, but realize that you may need to incur recruitment costs and incentives may need to be increased.

6. **Prepare the guide.** Put as much time into guide development as you would for paid projects. Include question types and activities that would intrigue observers.

7. **Run the session.** Consider recording real-time text chats to give a more realistic representation of the observer experience.

8. **Debrief observers.** These are your prospects. Meet individually with them to get their feedback and pursue next steps (an RFP).

9. **Re-purpose the demo as a case study.** Creatively re-package the demo to educate future prospects—those who were unable to observe the live demo.

Yes, it takes time and creativity to pull this off, but expenses can be controlled, and you'll have material that you can easily use in marketing to a wide range of prospects who may still be skeptical about the utility of online methods.

• VIDEO | TEXT CHAT | BOARD •

Tip B-6: Take Advantage of Platform Branding Options When Appropriate

Many online platforms allow the user to customize the look of the site—typically free of charge. The most basic level of customization replaces the platform provider's logo with either the researcher's or the end-client's name or logo. Higher levels of customization include adjusting the color scheme of the platform to reflect the brand colors and adding brand-related images or graphics to the landing page.

There are two situations when it makes sense to take advantage of this type of customization.

- **Non-Blinded Studies.** In this case, participants know who the study sponsor is. Assuming that participants in a non-blinded study already have an affinity for the sponsoring organization, seeing the platform not only can enhance the perceived legitimacy of the research but can strengthen participant's affinity for the brand.

- **Long-Term Communities.** In this case, the theme of the community can be showcased with graphics. Perhaps a logo for the community can be designed and included on all pages. Also, if it makes sense for the study sponsor to be identified, the name or logo of the organization that is sponsoring the community can be highlighted as well.

Since most projects are typically blinded, showcasing the name of the study sponsor will likely be counter-productive. Furthermore, it might actually be better to NOT highlight the research firm's or study sponsor's name. If technical issues arise (and they sometimes do . . . after all, NO online qual research platform is immune to hiccups), it's best for participants to associate those problems with the platform provider and not the researcher or the study sponsor.

2 | SELLING ONLINE QUALITATIVE

• VIDEO | TEXT CHAT | BOARD •

Tip B-7: Know that Online Qual is Not Necessarily Less Expensive Than In-Person

Those who have never moderated online focus groups or commissioned them are naturally curious about the cost of online projects versus in-person projects. A crude rule-of-thumb is that real-time online projects (video chats and text chats) will cost roughly the same as in-person projects, with the exception that there will be *zero travel costs* for the moderator and the observer team.

It's worth noting that depending on the number of observers, the number of markets, and the distances being traveled, the observer team's travel budget can be greater than the cost of the research itself! In that sense, online projects can cost significantly less than in-person projects.

What about asynchronous (multi-day) discussion boards? Roughly speaking, the cost of one discussion board will be equal to the cost of two in-person focus groups, two video chats, or two real-time text chats. The doubled cost is due to two major factors:

- **More participants per group**. Discussion boards can easily accommodate twice the number of participants as an in-person focus group. This will effectively double the number of participants, which directly impacts recruitment costs and incentive expenses.

- **More time needed to moderate.** Moderating an online discussion board requires more time than moderating an in-person group, a video chat, or a text chat. There are a lot more participants, each answering every question, and each providing much more detailed responses than are typically obtained in real-time groups. An attentive moderator should expect to spend at least 4 hours per day moderating a discussion board with 12–16 participants, where participants are each putting in 30–45 minutes of effort each day.

If a discussion board is being used for IDIs rather than a group discussion, budget 1–2 additional hours per day for moderating because there's even more to read. Participants are responding individually—not building on each other's comments. Also, many times the moderator of discussion-board IDIs will end up asking the same follow-up probes again and again; the time adds up.

Use these general rules of thumb to set expectations of those who are unfamiliar with the costs of online qualitative.

• VIDEO | TEXT CHAT | BOARD •

Tip B-8: Calculate Professional Services Costs Carefully

Whether you are a research supplier (self-employed or an employee of a larger research company) or a client-side researcher, you're probably responsible for estimating and managing project costs. For project management purposes, it's important for these estimates to be as accurate as possible. This tip should be used more as general rules of thumb, or as a "sanity check" when calculating your own estimates.

There are three categories of professional services work: study prep, data collection, and analysis and reporting.

Study Prep. This includes time spent in briefing meetings, screener development, moderator guide development, and general project management. When ballparking an estimate for a project, a good rule of thumb is to budget *at least* 8 hours for study prep. This assumes that the same guide will be used for all groups, and that there will be 2–4 groups in total. If it's a larger project or if different guides need to be developed for different groups, the number of hours will need to be increased.

Data Collection. This includes the time spent moderating or interviewing. Data collection time for real-time online projects is easy to estimate. Use the actual session length (usually 90 minutes) as a base, then add time for arriving at the group early to greet participants, time to debrief with the observer team afterward, and the time to download and adjust the transcript.

Data collection time for discussion boards is different. The very general rule-of-thumb is to budget 4 hours of moderating time per day per board. (See Tip A-7 for more details about moderator time for discussion boards.)

2 | SELLING ONLINE QUALITATIVE

- **Data Analysis.** This includes reporting and presentation time. Don't forget travel time if an in-person presentation is expected. Analysis time is roughly the same for in-person projects as for online projects. It is true that there is typically more data in text-based online options than either in-person groups or video chats, but transcripts in text-based projects are typically more coherent and organized, which offsets the increased amount of data that will need to be analyzed.

• BOARD •

TIP B-9: Watch the Time

When asked to provide cost estimates for discussion board projects, be sure to clarify whether the board is for individual interviews (IDIs) or interactive group discussions, because it will make a big difference in terms of how much time the moderator will require for the project. Knowing this up-front helps with scheduling, and helps assure that moderators get fairly compensated for their time spent on data collection.

Let's say that you have been asked to provide two cost estimates for a potential online discussion board project. One design option is for 16 IDIs (participants will never see each other's posts). The other design is for a fully interactive group discussion with 16 participants (they will see each other's posts as they come in). Assume that the same guide will be used in both designs, and that each board will be open for three days.

In terms of actual moderation time, one might think that the IDIs will take as much time as the interactive discussion board, because we will be asking the same number questions of the same number of participants. But the actual time spent moderating is likely to be greater for the IDIs than for the group discussion.

When boards are fully interactive, the moderator gains at least two efficiencies.

- When participants are able to see others' posts, some are likely to use a form of short-hand in their own posts. This shorthand naturally saves reading time for the moderator (and the other participants, too). Here are some examples:

- "Yes, I agree with most of the posts so far. In addition, . . . "
- "Ditto what A said."
- "I agree with what everyone said—especially in terms of _____.
  But I disagree with B about _____."

- If the moderator wants to probe several participants (or everybody) on a particular issue, they can ask the probing question once in an interactive discussion, instead of repeatedly needing to post the same probe for many individual participants in a board used for IDIs. This saves time as well.

For the same number of participants, a good rule-of-thumb is to expect to spend 25 percent more time moderating IDIs than an interactive group discussion.

SECTION 3

General Design Considerations

This section offers tips on how to navigate through the design process—methods selected, the number of interviews/groups to be conducted, and which platform provider to use. All have a direct impact on the final cost of an online qualitative project.

• VIDEO | TEXT CHAT | BOARD •

TIP C-1: Determine if Online is Appropriate

Sometimes a client will ask for in-person research when online might be better. At other times, online might be desired, but isn't the best solution. There are several ways to come to a clear sense of whether online or offline is better, or if both would be suitable.

The main question to ask is, "Will *seeing* respondents in-person be critical to the research?" If the answer is a definite YES, then it may be better to conduct in-person research. Here are some situations when in-person research is probably better:

- **Usability studies.** Usability research is one area where seeing respondents interact with *physical objects* may be important. Note that usability research with web-based stimuli like apps and websites can be effectively done online.

- **Taste tests.** There are situations when shelf-stable food products may be shipped to participants to consume at home. Some food products, however, need to be prepared in a certain way or served at a certain temperature; in such cases, in-person research at a facility is better.

- **Too-few prototypes available.** If there are product prototypes to be viewed by participants, and only a limited number have been produced, it may be unfeasible to conduct the research online.

35

- **Security risk.** If new concepts are extremely sensitive (proprietary), clients may be unwilling to allow them to be shared online out of fear that those ideas can get into the wrong hands.

- **Target audience is not tech-savvy.** Older individuals, as well as those in low socio-economic groups may not have, or be comfortable using smart phones, tablets, laptops, or desktop computers. In such cases, the best, option is to meet them in-person.

- **Need to get to know customers.** If one of the major objectives of the study is to help employees get to know their customers or potential customers, one can make an argument that in-person qualitative is better because it allows observers to get a fuller view of participants (albeit from behind a mirror).

In just about all other cases, online qualitative is likely to be a viable option to consider. Online is especially helpful in low-incidence situations, where there are so few people in a given market, making it nearly impossible to get them together for a group discussion. Some examples of low incidence groups would be those with a rare disease, C-suite employees in a particular industry or sub-industry, users of a particular high-end product, etc.

• VIDEO | TEXT CHAT | BOARD •

Tip C-2: Consider Mixed-Method Qualitative Research Approaches

When asked to suggest a design for qualitative projects, we typically think of using a single method. Thus, we'd suggest in-person focus groups OR online video chats OR online discussion boards, etc. Historically, single-method designs were preferred for their clean and simple approach. Today, though, it's often considered smarter to use a combination of methods to get more comprehensive insights.

All qualitative methods have their advantages and disadvantages. Some research goals might be better served using a combination of methods rather than just one method. Online methods are a good way to enable us to come up with a comprehensive solution.

Let's say we're doing a study for a luggage company. The goal is to find

3 | GENERAL DESIGN CONSIDERATIONS

opportunities to improve luggage for those who travel for business 50 or more nights per year. Among these frequent business travelers, we want to talk to a mix of super-frequent business travelers (100+ nights) and less-frequent travelers (50–99 nights per year). We have some doubts that the super-frequent travelers would be willing to participate. We can offer a different approach to reaching each segment.

- **In-person interviews for super-frequent travelers.** Because they are so time-strapped and always on-the-go, perhaps we can meet them at the airport before their flight. They can show us their luggage, evaluate it, and talk to us about unmet luggage needs. Logistically it will be costly to execute, and incentives will likely be high, but at least we'll gather insights from this very important group.

- **Discussion board IDIs with less-frequent travelers.** For less-frequent travelers, we can set up a discussion board that will be open for four weeks. As long as they have a business trip planned in that 4-week window, they should be able to participate. We will want them to take photos and perhaps a video or two while they are on the road, telling us about their luggage experiences.

Thus, both segments are handled. We don't have to force-fit one data collection approach to both groups. Online capabilities will come in very handy to reach out to the less-frequent traveler group.

• TEXT CHAT •

Tip C-3: Cap Text Chats at 90 Minutes

Moderators, participants, and observers begin to experience fatigue at around 90 minutes in a text chat. With eyes glued to a screen and fingers hovering over a keyboard for 90 continuous minutes, it's no wonder that online chats are physically more exhausting than in-person focus groups. It is for this reason that a best practice is that real-time text-based online chats should be no longer than 90 minutes.

We often find that what we accomplish in a 90-minute online chat would require two hours in an in-person focus group. How is this possible? The biggest factor which contributes to the speed of online chats is the fact that participants can all "talk" at the same time.

In an in-person focus group, participants tend to respectfully wait for somebody to finish speaking before they add to the dialog; it takes time for everybody to share their thoughts when they are shared sequentially. But there's no need to post sequentially in online chats. Everybody can type and post at the same time, saving a lot of time.

Of course, 90-minutes is not a hard-and-fast "rule" for online chats. Some chats are shorter, and some are longer. If an online chat is scheduled to take more than 90 minutes, we recommend giving participants a short break sometime after the half-way point of the discussion. When break time is called, encourage participants to take their hands off the keyboard and stretch their fingers, take their eyes off the screen and gaze out a window, or get up and move around and stretch. All of these are quick/easy ways to keep participants energized. These breaks can be short (1–3 minutes), yet quite refreshing.

• VIDEO | TEXT CHAT •

Tip C-4: Provide Ample Time for Breaks Between Real-Time Video and Text Chats

Both real-time online methods (text chats and video chats) can be physically demanding. The moderator, participants, and observers typically spend 90 minutes focusing on a screen. In the case of text chats, everybody pays close attention to rapidly scrolling text and hands ready to type most of the time. In the case of video chats, it's scrutinizing the faces on the screen and listening to what everyone is saying. The intensity of the experience can be exhausting, especially for the moderator who is charged with conducting a session shortly after completing another.

Between groups, fingers need a break from constantly hovering over a keyboard, eyes need a break from focusing intently at a computer monitor, and the brain needs to be put on pause for a while.

With this in mind, be sure to schedule a minimum of a 30-minute break between back-to-back sessions. Realize, though, that very little of that time is much of an actual break for the moderator, because in that brief period the moderator will likely do more than one of the following:

- Confer with observers to make sure all is going well.

3 | GENERAL DESIGN CONSIDERATIONS   39

- Make any needed changes to the guide before the next group.
- Be a good host by meeting with participants before the group begins.
- (If time permits) take a body break.

In the end, the moderator gets little (if any) actual down-time and for that reason should insist on a *minimum* of a 30-minute break. A truly refreshed moderator is a better moderator!

· BOARD ·

TIP C-5 Conduct International Discussions in Participants' Native Language

When an opportunity presents itself to do an international online qualitative project, find moderators who are fluent in the primary language used in the markets selected for research. As tempting as it may be to take the project on and moderate the groups in English (thinking that it'll be easy to find English-speaking respondents for your groups) resist the urge to do so. Using a moderator who is fluent in your participants' language is bound to not only be a more satisfying user experience for all involved, but the quality of the data generated is likely to be much higher as well.

I learned this lesson the hard way. In the early days of online qual (circa 2000), there were very few experienced online moderators who were fluent in languages other than English. Companies wanted to take advantage of the opportunity to conduct international research more economically via online methods (at the time, text-based methods only). Being generally restricted to doing online groups in English only, they were willing to focus on B2B research, because business decision-makers were more likely to be proficient in English.

In the screening process for those projects (almost always discussion boards because we wanted to enable participants to have plenty of time to understand the question and compose answers in their secondary language), we only invited those who professed being comfortable reading and writing in English. Unfortunately, this self-screening process did not work as well as hoped. Once the boards began, it was obvious that there were many levels of proficiency in English among the participants, and it was painfully disheartening to realize how many posts (in English) were almost useless even after posting follow-ups asking for clarification.

Fortunately, the online qualitative field has matured, and it is much easier to find skilled online moderators who are fluent in languages other than English. Expect this to get even easier as time goes on.

Platform providers are often able to help find such moderators who are fluent in other countries. The "Find a Moderator" function at *QRCA.org* is another resource for locating moderators who are fluent in languages other than English and skilled in online moderation.

• VIDEO | TEXT CHAT •

Tip C-6: Use Apps That Respondents Are Comfortable With

A good moderator puts participants at ease. Participants need to be comfortable if we want them to fully share their perceptions, opinions, beliefs, and attitudes on various topics. One way to help participants feel comfortable and engaged with online qualitative is to enable them to use online communication tools with which they are already familiar. Some examples:

- **Zoom.** With the COVID-19 pandemic, many consumers became familiar with Zoom. It's easier to recruit someone to a video chat on Zoom because it's likely to be a platform with which they have prior experience. Even if the platform to be used is not Zoom, telling recruits that it will be "Zoom-like" will set them at ease because they're familiar with it.

- **WhatsApp.** Among some demographic groups and in some geographies around the world, WhatsApp is very popular. If work is needed with those segments or geographies, using WhatsApp could make it easier to execute an online qualitative project because participants are already familiar with it.

- **"Text-like."** Texting is ubiquitous. It's a common form of communication among more and more people. Qualified recruits may not be familiar with a real-time text chat, but they certainly are familiar with texting. Telling them that a real-time text chat is nothing more than a group chat with strangers that is managed by a moderator is information they can relate to, making them more likely to be willing to participate.

Communication tools will continue to evolve. Be on the lookout for new communication devices or apps that gain popularity, because they might represent an opportunity to recruit audiences who might otherwise be difficult to reach.

· VIDEO ·

TIP C-7: Consider Video Chats for Research with Children

Don't rule out online video chats with young children. They can be quite effective.

In the 2000s, a client specified that they wanted me to moderate a set of video chats with children aged 5 to 7. The purpose was to get their reactions to concepts about kid-oriented food products. I was skeptical about whether we'd be able to get any actionable feedback via video chats.

The day for the groups came. The discussion progressed nicely, despite the fact that the kids' response to the first concepts was rather lukewarm. Then the third concept was presented to them, and it was as if a lightning bolt suddenly struck. Several kids immediately sat upright and moved closer to their screens. They wanted to be closer to the concept that caught their attention.

The lesson learned from that experience is that we shouldn't forget that kids can be more physically expressive than adults. They will physically get closer to things that appeal to them. This was clearly demonstrated on the moderator's screen, when all of a sudden there were a lot of close-ups of kids' faces!

Thus, while text-based chats and discussion boards represent challenges with kids as participants (especially younger ones, and their inability to articulate their feelings verbally in any detail), video chats are worth considering, even with children as young as 5 years old.

· BOARD ·

Tip C-8: Manage the Number of Discussion Board Participants

With traditional focus groups, we always over-recruit to make sure that enough will show up for a productive discussion. If more show than we agreed to seat in the focus group, we take those who we feel will best fit our needs, while the others are typically paid for their time, thanked, and sent home. The same process is typically used with online text chats as well as video chats.

But what about discussion boards? We still over-recruit to assure that a minimum number of participants will show. But with a discussion board we don't have the luxury of seeing who's going to participate until after the board launches and discussion begins.

We could maintain an open-door policy and admit all recruits who show up at the board. However, there are two potential drawbacks to this approach. First, too many participants can negatively impact interaction levels. Secondly, with more participants than expected, the amount of work for the moderator (reading and responding to posts) can increase beyond what was budgeted.

How can we control the number of participants in a discussion board? Here is one solution:

- Maintain the over-recruit strategy. We do not want to be disappointed by a response rate that is too low.
- Let all recruits know that more have been recruited than are needed, because we know that some will not be able to participate.
- Explain that despite over-recruitment, there is a maximum number of "seats" available at the board.
- Tell them that the board will be open to recruits on a first-come, first-served basis.
- Once the maximum number have begun posting, block access to the board by those who have not begun posting.

Here's a quick numerical example. Let's say we commit to recruiting 18 for 12–16 to show (16 is our maximum). We monitor logins and participation after the board launches. Once we reach 16 actively participating respondents, we close off access to the two who had not yet logged in.

This approach provides an incentive for participants to log in sooner than they otherwise might. At the same time, the recruiter is being fully transparent with participants, so that those who arrive too late should not be surprised or disappointed if they are ultimately not allowed to participate. In this case, we typically do not pay an incentive to those who are blocked, because they did not make any contribution to the discussion.

• BOARD •

Tip C-9: Schedule Discussion Boards Consecutively

When a study design calls for more than one online discussion board in a project, we need to decide how to schedule each board. Sometimes client demands dictate that the boards run concurrently to meet reporting deadlines. The obvious advantage of this is speed. However, there are downsides.

- **Burden on the moderator.** Moderating two (or sometimes more!) discussion boards at a time is physically exhausting.
- **Burden on observers.** Sometimes, needs of the client team will dictate that multiple boards need to be run at the same time to meet a reporting deadline. But it's tough to expect the client team to observe all boards that are running at the same time; it would be almost impossible for them to keep up, given other job responsibilities they are likely to have.

Ideally, discussion boards will be scheduled consecutively. In addition to putting less burden on both the moderator and the observer team, consecutive scheduling has another important benefit—**opportunities to improve the guide** over time. With in-person focus groups, we often learn things from one group (especially the first group) that lead to changes to the discussion guide in the next group. The same applies to discussion boards. After the first board, we are likely to learn things that convince us to make changes such as:

- Eliminating questions/activities that do not yield useful information.
- Revising activities to enable us to move more efficiently through a topic.
- Adding topics/questions to address unexpected issues raised by participants.
- Adding, deleting, replacing, or revising concepts based on participant feedback.

Of course, clients prefer projects to be completed sooner rather than later. Thus, they may not be willing to have multiple boards run consecutively (e.g., 3-day boards each running Tuesday–Thursday on consecutive weeks). If data collection time must be abbreviated, here are some options to consider for a project with three, 3-day boards. These suggestions focus on the welfare of the moderator.

- **Pause after first board.** Run the first board, make necessary changes, then launch the other boards. For example, Board 1 during Week 1 and Boards 2 and 3 at the same time during Week 2. This gives the research team time to more diligently think through what changes (if any) need to be made before Boards 2 and 3 launch.

- **Stagger start times.** Overlap boards, but have each one begin one day after the other. For example, one board can be run on Monday–Wednesday, a second can be run on Tuesday–Thursday, and the third on Wednesday–Friday. This is better than running them at the same time, because it at least gives the team a day to determine if changes are needed. It's a tight turn-around, but better than no rest period at all.

- **Multiple moderators.** Each moderator will take responsibility for one of the boards. This permits boards to be conducted concurrently. It will require close collaboration between the moderators in developing the guide and analyzing the results. The collaboration may add to the number of hours of professional time required of moderators working together, but it does permit greater speed.

- **Divide the observer team.** Divide the observation team into thirds

3 | GENERAL DESIGN CONSIDERATIONS

and have each team be responsible for observing just one of the three boards. Optionally, divide the topics up and assign them to different individuals or teams; each will focus on a particular topic (or topics) across all boards.

It's important to think through the implications and opportunities of various scheduling options. The pros and cons of each option should be discussed so that the team can make an informed decision.

• BOARD •

Tip C-10: Establish Capacity Limits in Discussion Boards

Just as you would do with in-person groups, over-recruit for discussion boards to assure that you get a minimum number of recruits to actually show and participate. It's easy to handle a higher-than-expected show rate in an in-person focus group or for any real-time online chat—you pick who to keep and then excuse (with pay) the others. It's not as easy to deal with a too-high show rate in a discussion board because discussion board participants don't all show up at the same time.

You might say, "Why not accept everyone who shows? That's more data for the project, which is a good thing. Right?" Yes, more data is a good thing, but the more participants there are in a discussion board that's intended for group discussion, there's a lot more to read and react to—for participants, observers, and the moderator. Too many participants in a discussion board that's set up for group discussion can have a negative impact on participants' ability and willingness to interact with others.

There's a way to control the number of participants in a discussion board, even when we over-recruit. Here's what to do if you recruit more than the maximum you want to be part of the group discussion.

- **Be transparent.** Let recruits know that you are over-recruiting and why. Let them know that once the board launches, you will accept x number of participants into the board on a first-come, first-served basis. After that, late-comers will not be able to participate. This tactic encourages them to begin posting earlier than they might otherwise start.

- **Monitor.** Scrutinize how many participants begin posting on the first day. Be especially watchful as the number of participants approaches the maximum number you're willing to admit.
- **Block.** If and when the limit is reached, turn off access to those who have not logged in and began posting.
- **Inform.** Send a note to those whose access has been blocked, letting them know what's been done, and why. Of course, thank them for agreeing to participate and encourage them to accept future invitations to other online group discussions.

By taking these simple steps, you're more likely to get the minimum number of participants you hope for. At the same time you, as well as participants and observers, won't be overwhelmed with extra data generated by too many participants, and you can control the amount that will need to be spent on incentives.

· BOARD ·

Tip C-11: Determine if the Layout of a Discussion Board Platform Will Be Suitable

When using a discussion board for an interactive discussion—where participants see others' responses and you want them to interact with each other—note that some platform designs are more likely to foster interaction.

There are two general ways that replies to questions may be presented in a board. We refer to the two options as "Flat" and "Indented."

Here's an example of an "Indented" presentation of ten posts.

- (Post #1) Moderator's Question
- (Post #2) Participant 1's Response
- (Post #3) Participant 2's Response
    - ○ (Post #5) Moderator's Follow-up to Participant 2's Response
        - – (Post #9) Participant 2's Response to Moderator's Follow-Up
    - ○ (Post #7) Participant 3's Reply to Participant 2's Response
        - – (Post #10) Participant 2's Reply to Participant 3
- (Post #4) Participant 3's Response

3 | GENERAL DESIGN CONSIDERATIONS   47

- ○ (Post #6) Participant 1's Reply to Participant 3's Response
- (Post #8) Participant 4's Response
- Etc.

With indenting, posts that go together are visually nested (threaded) together, making it easy for participants to 1) follow who's talking to whom and 2) make a meaningful addition to the conversation.

Now, here is the same discussion presented in a "Flat" view. All responses are shown in the order in which they were posted. The participant is forced to figure out who is talking to whom, which acts as a natural barrier to engaging with others.

- (Post #1) Moderator's Question
- (Post #2) Participant 1's Response
- (Post #3) Participant 2's Response
- (Post #4) Participant 3's Response
- (Post #5) Moderator's Follow-up Question to Participant 2
- (Post #6) Participant 1's Reply to Participant 3's Response
- (Post #7) Participant 3's Comment to Participant 2's Response
- (Post #8) Participant 4's Response
- Etc.

The flat view is perfectly fine if you are doing IDIs on a discussion board, because they only see the moderator's questions and follow-up, and their own responses. However, if the discussion board project is intended to generate interaction among participants, it's likely that you will see more interaction on an indented board than on a flat board. Keep this in mind when selecting a platform for your discussion board study.

One more important note. Some platform providers only provide the indented format on their desktop/laptop versions and NOT on the mobile app versions of their platform. Once again, if interaction is important in your project, check out what the user experience will be like on different devices. You may want to switch platforms, or you may need to recruit only those who will be able to participate on a non-mobile device.

• BOARD •

TIP C-12: Anticipate Whether Break Days in Discussion Boards Would Be Helpful

We all need breaks once in a while. Breaks help us to re-energize and be more productive. Breaks are an option to consider in discussion boards— especially those that are longer than three days. Here are some ways in which breaks can be used:

- **Schedule a Day Off in the Middle of the Board.** Add a day to the data collection period, but allow one day in the middle of the board to serve as a "break day" which will provide those who have fallen behind to catch up, and will reward those who have managed to keep up with an unexpected day off. Don't tell participants in advance that there will be a break day, surprise them with the news at the end of the day before the break day.

- **Schedule an Optional Extra Discussion Day at the End.** Whatever the anticipated number of required days for the discussion, add one more day at the end. For example, if the board is scheduled to last three days, tell participants that it will last four days. Once Day 3 is over, the following can happen:

  ○ If all participants have answered all questions, announce that the group finished faster than planned and close the board at the end of Day 3. Participants are happy because the board turns out to be one day shorter than planned.

  ○ The extra day can be left open for those who weren't able to finish their work by the end of Day 3. The fourth day serves as a "safety net" for those who fall behind. Those who completed their work on Day 3 get Day 4 off.

  ○ If additional issues arise that the team did not anticipate, Day 4 is available to explore them. The team is happy to get more data, and participants fulfill the number of days they were told the board would last.

- **Give Everyone a Chance to Participate.** In longer-term communities, it's often recommended to "pulse" activities (for example, once a

3 | GENERAL DESIGN CONSIDERATIONS   49

week), to give all community members an opportunity to participate on days that are convenient to them. They have more flexibility
in terms of when to answer that day's questions.

- **Merge Two Projects into One.** For example, consider the need to
develop concepts for quantitative testing. Traditionally, we would
run a set of groups to identify gaps in current product/service offer-
ings. Once the team uses the feedback to develop potential concepts to address those gaps, a second set of groups are run (with
new participants) to evaluate the concepts. With the convenience of
discussion boards, we can use the same participants in both phases.
They get a break (ideally no more than a week) between the two
phases. They're fresh, they know one another a bit, and they get
to be more involved in the product/service development process.
Because we don't need to recruit a separate set of respondents for
Phase 2, recruitment costs are reduced.

• VIDEO | TEXT CHAT | BOARD •

Tip C-13: Opt for Real Names Whenever Possible

Most online qualitative research platforms enable project managers to
control the participant names that appear on the screen. Just as with
in-person groups, we typically use participant first names only, and add
a last initial only if there is more than one participant with the same first
name in the group. By allowing participants to appear using their own
name, they are more likely to be themselves. They are less likely to take
on a different persona and share a point-of-view that is not their own.

There are situations, however, when having participants use their real
names in group discussions (not IDIs) may compromise the integrity of
the research. Here are some examples:

- **Employees.** In employee satisfaction research, participants may be
hesitant to criticize the organization if other participants or observers know who they are.

- **Competitors.** Some B2B focus groups may include representatives
from competing organizations, e.g., purchasing agents for law firms.
In such cases, participants may be reluctant to share what they
consider to be confidential information.

- **Politics.** In political research in smaller communities where participants are more likely to know at least one of the other participants,
  some may be uncomfortable sharing an unpopular thought or
  opinion on a hot issue.

In such instances, the use of "aliases" (also called pseudonyms) will
preserve the anonymity of participants, thereby allowing them to be as
open as possible in the discussion. In addition, video chats are ill-advised
because seeing and hearing participants, even with an alias, are no longer anonymous.

Aliases can be anything that sounds neutral (e.g., types of trees: ma-
ple, oak, aspen, etc.; colors: red, green, yellow, etc.; types of pets: cat, dog,
fish, etc.). We recommend shying away from using aliases that may be
perceived to be "better" than others (e.g., country names: Russia vs. U.S.;
states/provinces: California vs. Alabama; cities: San Francisco vs. Balti-
more; animals: snake vs. koala; brands: Chevrolet vs. Tesla).

SECTION 4

Recruitment

This section is all about how to find participants, what to say to them about the online experience, and how to address any questions or issues they may have before they even ask them.

• VIDEO | TEXT CHAT | BOARD •

Tip D-1: Consider an Automated + Manual Recruitment Process

For most online qualitative projects, recruitment is usually handled online. It's an automated process, that typically proceeds in the following way:

STEP 1   An online panel company is selected.

STEP 2   A screener is developed and programmed for completion online.

STEP 3   The panel company sends a text or email to a portion of its database that fits the basic criteria (e.g., 21–39-year-old females within a certain geography). The message includes a link to the screener.

STEP 4   The panelist completes the screener to see if they qualify.

STEP 5   The system thanks the panelist for their time if they do not qualify.

STEP 6   If the panelist qualifies, the system provides details about the project (dates/times, incentive, etc.), and invites the panelist to opt-in.

STEP 7   The panelist accepts or rejects the invitation to participate.

STEP 8   The system closes off quota groups (e.g., those with or without children in the household) as they are filled, minimizing over-recruitment.

This automated process is all that's needed in most cases. Sometimes, though, there are screening requirements that require human judgment for qualities like articulation and subject-matter expertise. By adding a manual step to the automated process, the recruitment process can be refined to find who we really need. In this case, we follow Steps 1–6 above, then branch off in the following way:

NEW STEP 7	Inform the panelist that before they can be accepted, they must complete an additional task (sometimes for a small incentive, if appropriate), such as . . . • **Answer an open-end question.** This can be used to assess the strength of their communication skills or their knowledge/expertise in a particular topic or product category. • **Upload a photo or two.** This can be used to verify that they own certain products or to see how willing and able they are to complete photo-taking activities in the project. • **Post a video response.** This might be done to assess subject matter expertise or to see if they are willing to record and submit a video response—important if video clips are needed for the report.
NEW STEP 8	Panelists are informed *when* they should hear back about their status, *who* will contact them, and by *when* they should hear back.
NEW STEP 9	Evaluations of these extra screener activities are completed by one or more members of the research team.
NEW STEP 10	The panelist is informed that they do not qualify, or they are invited to opt-in to the study, and accepts or rejects the invitation to participate.

The combination of an automated screener with human evaluation of feedback to any additional activities can help locate the best participants for a particular project. There will be additional costs because of the human element required.

• VIDEO | TEXT CHAT | BOARD •

TIP D-2: Manage Respondent Expectations During Recruitment

Online qualitative research is still new to many participants. Don't let participants get caught off guard; be fully transparent with them about what they should expect. As part of the recruitment process, it is important to clearly state the requirements of their participation so that they can make an informed decision about whether to accept the invitation to participate. It's not a bad idea to explain twice about how things will work—once when they are initially recruited, and again when reminder messages are sent out.

4 | RECRUITMENT

The requirements of participants in online qual vary by the type of online research being conducted (i.e., real-time text chat, discussion board, video chat). Here is a short list of what to include in the recruitment process before asking them to participate.

Discussion Boards

- Specify the dates of the board to make sure they are available on all days.
- Tell them how much time they should expect to spend on the board each day (typically 30–60 minutes per day).
- Detail requirements, if any, about number of times a day they must participate, or desired hours (time blocks) for participation.
- Emphasize that if they do not respond to all questions on all days, they forfeit their incentive. We typically pay a partial incentive if they complete at least one day, but this statement puts pressure on them to fully participate.
- If the board will be set up as a group discussion, tell them that they are expected to interact with other participants.

Real-Time Text Chats

- Tell them there will be NO video, and NO audio. Say that it will be like texting with a group of people simultaneously, with a discussion leader.
- Explain that there will be other participants (up to 8) and that they are expected to interact with the other participants.
- Emphasize that they will be expected to answer all of the moderator's questions.
- If the platform to be used is not optimized for mobile devices, stress that they must participate with a laptop or desktop.

Video Chats

- Explain that it will be very much like work or personal video chats they may have participated in since the pandemic began.
- If the video chat will be a group discussion, let them know that they MUST participate on a tablet, laptop, or desktop. Emphasize

that we need participants to see each other and interact, which is difficult to do on the small screen of a smart phone.

- If the video chat will be for an IDI, tell them that they can participate with a smartphone, but stipulate that they must NOT drive during the interview.

A fully-informed participant will be better prepared, more likely to show up, and hopefully more engaged as well.

• VIDEO | TEXT CHAT | BOARD •

TIP D-3: Relieve Any Respondent Anxieties

Some first-time recruits for online qualitative projects are reticent to participate because it will be too-foreign of an experience. There are several things that can be done to set respondents at ease.

- **Positive Spin.** During recruitment, when they are invited to participate, stress that the experience will be *easy* and *fun*. Otherwise, fear about the task being mundane or difficult can serve as a barrier to agreeing to participate.

- **Offer Back-Up.** Assure them that Tech Support will be available if needed at any time.

- **Pre-Session Login.** Send login instructions in advance and ask them to log in prior to the group to confirm that everything is set. Even if the room is not open, having "kicked the tires" gives them a sense of accomplishment and solidifies their commitment to participate. They will be less likely to "chicken out" and be a no-show.

• VIDEO | TEXT CHAT | BOARD •

Tip D-4: Decide Which Devices Participants Should Use to Effectively Participate

Mobile phones are ubiquitous. For a growing percentage of people, a smartphone is their only access to the internet. This has implications for online qualitative projects. If a smartphone's screen size is considered to be too small for participants to easily see what they need to see, then smartphones may need to be ruled out as a device to use for a given project. Thus, if smartphones are unsuitable for a particular study, include a screener question about devices the prospective participant has available; if they only have a smartphone, exclude them from the study.

Video Chats. Tablets, laptops, and desktops are all suitable for video chats of up to six participants (plus the moderator). When it comes to smartphones, however, the screen size is usually too small to see more than two participants (plus the moderator). If the point is to see each other, the screen size needs to be sufficiently large. In fact, when it comes to video chats, some may argue that smartphones should be used only for IDIs (1-on-1 interviews) and not group chats.

Real-Time Text Chats. A text chat platform provider may or may not have optimized their platform for smartphones. In addition, in a fast-moving text chat, participants may miss part of the conversation because the chat stream scrolls up too fast for them to keep up. They may scroll back to see something they missed, only to be forced down to the bottom of the thread as soon as another post comes in; this can be very frustrating for the participant. Check with the platform provider or ask for a demo to confirm that a smartphone will be suitable for participants to use for text chats.

Discussion Boards. Some discussion board platform providers display posts in a visual way that makes it easy to see who's responding to whom, to intuitively understand the thread of the discussion. This is more important in interactive group discussions where multiple people are "talking" to each other. Also, some discussion boards on a mobile device will hide the question when the participant goes to reply to it; this creates a less-than-optimized user experience. In general, I often advise participants to use a laptop/desktop as their primarily device for discussion boards, and that a mobile device should be used only as a back-up device.

Thus, there are two things that the researcher should do in planning an online study.

- Think through whether smaller devices will enable participants to *easily* and *effectively* participate. If the answer is "No," only accept those who can participate on a larger device.
- If all device types are deemed suitable for the project, it is still

recommended to evaluate the mobile device version to determine if the user experience will be minimally acceptable. Choose a platform provider who offers a decent user experience regardless of the device type used.

• VIDEO | TEXT CHAT | BOARD •

Tip D-5: Reinforce the Need to Use Particular Devices to Participate

Wouldn't it be great if participants were able to fully and effectively participate in online qualitative projects with whatever device they choose? Unfortunately, some devices won't work well in some circumstances.

Smartphones are both popular and useful, but they are not always suitable for online focus groups. Still, even though a recruit gets invited because they have a laptop or desktop to participate, they may decide at the last minute to log on with a smartphone.

When it's decided that the limitations of smartphones will handicap participants' ability to easily see each other or read others' posts, use the following three-step approach to make sure that all participants know that they must use another tool to participate.

1. **Screener stage.** Include a screener question asking which devices they have ready access to (smartphone, tablet, laptop, or desktop). If they only have access to a smartphone, screen them out of the study. (This was covered in Tip D-4.)

2. **Reminder stage.** When reminder notices are sent out, double-check that they still plan on participating using a tablet, laptop, or desktop. If their situation has changed (e.g., no longer able to participate at home on their desktop and will only have a smartphone to use), they should be excused.

3. **As the session begins.** Some may not believe that smartphones won't work well. As they begin to show up for the session, ask what kind of device they are using at the moment. If they are using a smartphone, ask them to switch to a device with a larger screen. If they are unable to do so in a timely fashion, excuse them.

The above steps help ensure that all participants are able to comfortably see/hear/read other participants and fully interact with them. It's

4 | RECRUITMENT

wasteful in a real-time discussion (video chat or text chat) to have to excuse someone in the middle of a session because it becomes clear that they are using a device that hampers their ability to fully participate.

• TEXT CHAT •

Tip D-6: Maximize Show Rates in Real-Time Chats

As with in-person focus groups, we over-recruit for online focus groups to make sure that we have enough people show and participate to constitute a quorum. At the same time, we don't want to over-recruit too much because we prefer to not over-spend on recruitment costs and incentive payments. Here's how to manage how much to over-recruitment:

- **Make phone a key part of the recruitment process.** Without some sort of verbal commitment by the recruit to the recruiter, it's more likely that recruits will not show. Email notifications are impersonal. Speaking live to the recruiter is ideal, but even hearing a recorded message from the recruiter stressing the importance of the recruit's presence can boost show rates.

- **Send at least two phone reminders.** Recruits need to be constantly reminded of their commitment to participate. If you are using phone reminders, the first should be sent at least a few days prior to the group. The second should be sent on the day of the scheduled group, several hours before the chat launches.

- **If email reminders are used, increase the number of reminders and require a response.** If there is no phone contact with the recruit, schedule at least three email reminders: 1) a few days before the group, 2) 24 hours in advance, and 3) one more time several hours prior to the launch of the group. Tell recruits to acknowledge receipt of the reminder and confirm their commitment to participate.

- **Offer fair incentives.** To maximize show rates, don't skimp on incentives; offer as much as would be offered for in-person groups. If there is any uncertainty about how much to offer, trust the recruiter to provide guidance in this area.

- **Pay all who show.** Even if not all who show can be accepted into a group, pay those who show on time. Do as we do for in-person groups—pay the full incentive to all who show on time, whether they are accepted into the group or sent home.

We find that when we follow the guidelines above, we don't have to over-recruit any more for our online groups than we do for in-person groups. The result is a win-win for everyone: the project gets executed as planned, no make-up groups need to be scheduled, and participants feel they are treated fairly.

• VIDEO | TEXT CHAT | BOARD •

Tip D-7: Harness the Power of Reminder Calls

Brick-and-mortar facilities have traditionally used telephone reminder calls to maximize the show rate for in-person focus groups and IDIs. When a recruit makes a verbal promise to the recruiter over the phone that they will show for the interview or group, their likelihood of actually showing up increases markedly.

We live in a web-based world where a lot of communication takes place by text and email. With that in mind, it would seem that recruits for online focus groups who are often recruited via online surveys don't need a telephone reminder call. But based on experience, this is not the case. Online panel companies that do not include telephone reminders in the recruitment process may need to recruit 3 to 4 times the number of people needed to fill a group. This approach is risky. What if we recruit 24 for 8 to show, and 16 show up? The expense of the incentives paid for those who show but are not admitted into the main discussion area can be quite high.

When the online recruitment process includes a telephone reminder call, we seldom need to over-recruit more than we would for in-person groups. When a recruit for an online focus group gets a phone call asking them to confirm their participation, the recruit is impressed that someone has taken the time and effort to reach out to them. That phone call makes them feel that their participation is *really* important. Even if a voice message needs to be left with the recruit, hearing a human voice asking them to confirm their participation helps solidify their commitment to actually show.

Here is an example of what might be communicated in these reminder calls:

"Hi, my name's [X]. This is a friendly reminder about an online focus group that you agreed to participate in on [date/time]. You should have received an email with instructions for how to log in. If you haven't, please phone or text me, and we'll take care of it. Please phone or text back to confirm your attendance. We're counting on your participation."

Here are two anecdotes to illustrate the importance of reminders by phone.

Anecdote A

I had been subcontracted by a large market research supplier to moderate a real-time chat group. The supplier's online panel partner took care of recruitment. Recruitment happened entirely online, and 24 qualified recruits agreed to participate. The panel company and the supplier were confident that with 24 recruits we would easily get a group of 6–8 to show. At least four reminder emails were sent to all recruited participants prior to the scheduled session. Recruits were asked to let the recruiter know if they would not be able to make it. Nobody responded that they would not be able to attend.

How many showed? ONE. At ten minutes after the scheduled start time, and with still only one participant, the session was cancelled. This understandably frustrated the observer team because so much time was wasted for virtually nobody to arrive.

What explains the extremely poor show rate? There were no weather issues or any other type of event to explain the poor show rate, and incentives were a standard amount. The most reasonable explanation for the low show rate was the failure to secure a firmer commitment from recruits prior to the session.

Anecdote B

In another study, I was contracted to complete around 30 video IDIs. These were hard-to-find, somewhat transient individuals. It was considered safer to recruit 40 to get 30 completes.

How many showed? 38. Eight more than needed!

What explains the beyond expectations show rate? One factor was the high incentive rate—nearly double what normally would be paid for a 45-minute video chat. But another key factor became apparent in a conversation I had with one of the recruiters. She told me that she talked to them in great depth about the purpose of the study, how it would work, and how important the project was for the study sponsor. Not only did she speak in great depth, but she talked to each recruit several times. Thus, it appears that the actual phone calls played a big role in the recruitment success of this project.

When getting proposals for recruitment of online projects, be sure to ask if phone reminder calls are included. The added expense of these reminder calls is typically well worth it.

• VIDEO •

Tip D-8: Coach Video Chat Participants on How to be Helpful

Since the pandemic, many people have participated in video chats for business or personal use. Especially in the first year of the pandemic, we all witnessed rather chaotic video chats.

Fortunately, video chats these days run more smoothly because many have learned the "etiquette" of participating in them. Still, to optimize video-chat focus groups, we should properly prep our participants. Begin prepping them during recruitment. Follow up with an email or reminder call to offer advice. Bottom line: get them prepared before the scheduled video chat session so that minimal chat session time is spent on logistics.

Here are some tips to share with video-chat participants before the focus group:

- **No distractions.** Ask them to participate from a quiet spot, not a place where kids are playing, or where other household members are watching TV, airport terminals, while shopping, while driving, etc.

- **Self-mute as needed.** Not all participants can find a distraction-free zone. If that's the case, advise them to mute themselves when they know when audible distractions occur (barking dogs, screaming kids, roaring overhead planes, etc.). Otherwise, ask them to leave their mic on to foster a more free-flowing discussion.

- **Stay still.** Unless we need participants to move to another area, we want them to sit still. Ask them to place their device in front of them on a stable surface (NOT their lap!).

- **Proper lighting.** Ask participants to avoid being back-lit. During daylight hours, they should be facing a window rather than having the window behind them. When lights are on, they should be facing the light. We don't want silhouettes.

- **Interrupt gently.** Ask them to interject when nobody else is talking. Explain that only one voice is heard when two or more speak at the same time. Encourage them to raise their hand and wait to be called on.

- **Have pen and paper on hand.** They may want to take notes during the session, or you may want them to write something down before discussing it. Rather than taking time to leave the screen to find paper and something to write with, ask them ahead of time to have it on hand.

- **Keep bandwidth use under control.** This applies only when there may be three or more internet users in a household while a video chat takes place. If video concepts are to be shown, or if high quality video clips are needed for the report, advise recruits to ask those using the same internet connection to lighten up their use of high-bandwidth activities (like gaming, streaming movies, etc.) while the video-chat focus group is going on.

Be sure that participants are given these tips beforehand, to maximize the time spent on actual discussion and minimize time spent on dealing with logistics during the session. As needed, quickly review these guidelines at the beginning of the video-chat session.

• VIDEO | TEXT CHAT | BOARD •

Tip D-9: Protect Client Intellectual Property

Whenever we use qualitative research to collect feedback about proprietary ideas or product prototypes, it's important to make sure that participants don't share those ideas outside of the qualitative discussion. As a standard operating procedure, many brick-and-mortar focus group facilities ask recruits to sign a non-disclosure agreement (NDA) when they arrive at the facility. The NDA requires that they not share with anybody outside the focus group anything that was shown or discussed during the group. Rarely do participants refuse to sign; if they do refuse to do so, they are not admitted into the discussion.

It's easy to get signed NDAs for in-person groups, and it's easy to accomplish this for online discussions and interviews as well. Here are three ways to do it.

GOOD. At the beginning of an online chat, the NDA is presented to participants on their screens; they are given an opportunity to read it over and asked to signal their agreement with it. If they don't agree, the moderator excuses them before the chat begins. *The downside of this option is that it puts the recruit "on the spot" and they may not truly realize what they are committing to. It may also "scare" them and cause us to lose a valuable recruit.*

BETTER. Platform providers may be able to insert a step in the login process, requiring the participant to agree to an NDA. If they don't agree, their access to the platform is blocked. *This option is fine for discussion boards because there is no rush to get the NDA signed. But in the case of real-time text or video chats, if a participant shows up at the last minute, they may feel rushed and skeptical about what they are being asked to agree to. Or, if they show up at the last minute and decide to scrutinize the NDA, the start of the discussion may be delayed.*

BEST. A recruiter can email an NDA to the recruit and require them to sign and return it before the group begins. With no signed NDA, they don't get access to the online platform. *The advantage of this procedure is that it's done well in advance of the launch of the project, giving the recruit plenty of time to understand what they are committing to.*

It's a good idea at the end of an online session to remind participants of their agreement to not share any info about the focus group with anyone outside of the discussion.

In summary, protect your client's intellectual property, and protect yourself. Issue an NDA whenever client intellectual property is at stake and send a copy of the NDA to participants to remind them of their agreement.

• VIDEO | TEXT CHAT •

Tip D-10: Plan Carefully for Online Focus Groups with Employees

Some organizations conduct focus groups with employees. Examples include employee satisfaction, or getting feedback about potential changes in the company.

Real-time text chats and video chats may be deemed more attractive for employee focus groups because they require less time of employees. Of these two options, text chats may be considered better because participant anonymity (all text, no voice or video) can be maximized.

It might be difficult to get sufficient numbers of employees to participate in text or video chats. Here are eight tips to maximize the success of online focus groups with employees.

1. **Get Management to Sanction Participation.** Have senior executives communicate their support of the study, encouraging employees to participate.

2. **Offer Incentives.** Give participants time off to participate during work, or offer comp time if they participate after work hours. Cash incentives are another option. Employees may be loyal to their employer, but money talks, just as it does for recruits in most market research.

3. **Address Possible Technology Issues.** If recruits can participate from work, be sure that firewalls will not prevent them from accessing the online focus group platform. If stimuli will be shown with sound, or if video chats are conducted, be sure that there are no policies in place that prohibit speakers being used on any type of computer (some organizations do this to control workplace noise levels).

4. **Over-Recruit.** Always recruit more employees than needed, because it is rare that everyone who's been recruited will show up. Work respon-

sibilities may get in the way of participation, or a recruit may call in sick that day.

5. **Be Transparent About Over-Recruitment.** If there will be a limit of how many participants can be accepted, state this up-front so there are no surprises.

6. **Maximize anonymity.** If there is any concern that participants knowing each other will affect how they respond to questions, then strike video chats from consideration and assign an alias (fake name) to each participant.

7. **Send Reminders.** Be sure to send reminder notices leading up to the session, to maximize the probability that they will actually show up and show up on time.

8. **Stick to Time Limits.** Do not spend more time than promised. Thus, if you say it will be a 90-minute discussion, do not go over 90 minutes.

Doing all of the above will maximize show-rates and the chance that your online chat sessions with employees will go flawlessly.

SECTION 5

Discussion Guides

In some ways, discussion guides are more important in text-based interviews and groups, such as real-time text chats and multi-day discussion boards, than for in-person sessions and even video chats. Every word counts! Guides for text chats and boards are markedly different than guides for in-person and video sessions. This section offers tips to make guides the best they can be.

• VIDEO | TEXT CHAT | BOARD •

Tip E-1: Appreciate the Value of a Thorough Warm-Up

Whether online or in-person, it's important to provide an opportunity for participants to warm-up. Because online groups are not as personal or intimate as in-person groups, one could argue that it's even *more important* to permit some warm-up time in online sessions to give participants a chance to get comfortable with each other.

The five steps to warm-up a group are the same for online and in-person groups. The moderator should:

1. Welcome everyone, introduce themself, explain their role, and announce the general topic.
2. Explain how the session will work.
3. Provide guidelines.
4. Ask participants to introduce themselves.
5. "Close the circle" by answering the same warm-up questions about themselves.

Just as with in-person groups, it's good to keep the self-introductions short, with no more than 3–4 questions for participants to quickly and easily answer. It's helpful to include a question that is in some way

65

connected to the study topic. If appropriate, a fun question could also be included to keep the tone light at this early stage of the discussion.

Here are some additional notes about the self-introductions:

- There's no need to ask participants to say their name in real-time text chats or discussion boards, because the system will show their name on every post.

- While participant names will show on the screen in video chats, it's important to ask participants to state their name so all hear how their name is pronounced.

- In real-time text chats, ask participants to complete their self-intro in a single post. Otherwise, if they use separate posts to answer all parts of the self-intro, it will be difficult to get a holistic impression of who the person is.

- In discussion boards, it's okay to ask for longer self-introductions than might be asked for in-person groups, because there's no rush in a discussion board.

- In any online session, consider asking participants to state where they live. If all participants are from one metro area, they realize that everyone is a "neighbor." If they are from different parts of the country (or from different countries), they get a sense of how geographically diverse the group is.

The more quickly online participants can be made comfortable with the moderator and their fellow participants, the more engaged they will be, and the more forthcoming they will be in revealing their perceptions, opinions, beliefs, and attitudes.

Yes, the time spent on this warm-up activity takes time away from gathering data on the end-client's important issues. Clients would love to skip over the warm-up and start collecting "real" data as soon as the group begins. But it is time well-spent because the warm-up process does exactly that; it gets the participants ready to hit the ground running when the first main topic of discussion is raised.

5 | DISCUSSION GUIDES

• TEXT CHAT | BOARD •

TIP E-2: Mix it Up

This tip serves as a reminder of best practices in all qualitative data-gathering settings, but applies primarily to text-based online methods (real-time text chats and discussion boards). The idea is to create as pleasant a participant experience as possible. The more participants enjoy the online research experience, the more productive your online focus group will be.

- **Take a Poll.** If the platform you are using has a polling feature, take advantage of it. In an online chat, polls are useful for getting respondents to commit to an answer without being influenced by others. It's the same as having respondents write down their answers before sharing and discussing them during in-person groups. Remember that because this is qualitative research, polls should be used as a conversation starter—NOT as a quantitative test.

- **Vary Your Verbiage.** Make your questions as conversational as possible. Change your question stems. You could ask these three questions in a row: "What do you think about X? . . . What do you think about Y? . . . What do you think about Z?" But doesn't it come across a little more warmly the following way: "What do you think about X? . . . Let's turn our attention now to Y. What are your thoughts about it? . . . And finally, how does Z compare to the first two?"

- **Elicit Different Response Lengths.** Respondents are spending a lot of time on the keyboard while they're participating. They appreciate little breaks. You can do this by tossing in an easy yes/no or other very short-answer type of question. It gives them time to rest their fingers, and makes them more motivated to spend a bit more time on questions that require longer responses.

- **Show Things.** Give your respondents some visual relief on their screen. Use the whiteboard to show keywords that help them focus on a new part of the discussion. Perhaps show an image that's related to the current topic. If you're doing a concept test, show the concept in the whiteboard.

- **Use Interventions.** Projective exercises allow respondents to get out of their own skin. Showing a set of ambiguous images in the whiteboard and having them pick one that fits their feeling about an issue/brand/idea/etc. is a nice diversion. Show them a list of words and have them pick the ones that they most relate to on a particular issue.

These are just some of the ways that you can keep things fresh for your respondents and help get the most out of your text-based online focus groups.

• VIDEO | TEXT CHAT | BOARD •

Tip E-3: Use Polls to Help Participants Focus

Most online qualitative platforms (real-time text chats, real-time video chats, and discussion boards) have a polling feature, which allows the moderator to ask a survey-type question with closed-end response options. The moderator also has control over whether participants can see others' responses before posting their own response, and the moderator can also control whether to allow only one answer or more than one response to a question.

While survey questions are a no-no in qualitative research (online as well as in-person), if used properly, they can help steer and propel discussions. Here are some examples of polling questions:

- Which of the four concepts I showed you is most appealing to you?
- Pick up to three of the items on this list which best explain your reluctance to use X?
- Which of the following statements is best at encouraging you to try product Y?

Because polls are a novelty in qualitative discussions, they energize participants. Polls are easy to do because participants simply pick a response, and they're quick because they are faster than typing a response. If the moderator shows a graph of the poll results, participants can see how the whole group "voted."

As with all qualitative, the results of polls should not be included in reports. However, in the context of a given group, the results are a perfect launching pad for further insightful discussion. Here are some examples:

- I see that most of you picked X. What is it about X that made it the "winner" in this group?
- Why do you suppose nobody in this group picked Y?
- How would you change Idea Z to help it get picked over the other Ideas?

Take advantage of polls to engage your participants, get quick feedback on a particular issue, and to help you decide which follow-up probes to ask next.

• VIDEO | TEXT CHAT | BOARD •

TIP E-4: Beware of Client-Provided Discussion Guides

Clients may sometimes ask a moderator to bid on a project with the caveat, "Don't worry about the guide. We'll take care of that." They may think they are doing us a favor (and saving themselves money) by providing us with the discussion guide, but I've NEVER seen a discussion guide from a client that could not benefit from my input. Some of the things I find myself doing with a supposedly "finished" guide from clients include:

- **Rearrange topics.** Re-arranging the topic flow or sequence of questions to better fit the information objectives.
- **Make it sound more conversational.** Building in preambles and transitions to make the guide feel more "human" and less "robotic."
- **Simplify the language.** Converting client jargon into consumer language.
- **Add activities.** Adding exercises that take advantage of the particular capabilities of the online platform to be used.
- **Assess time requirements.** Informing the client that they have underestimated how much time it will take to get through the guide.

Many clients, and also qualitative researchers with no online moderating experience, mistakenly believe that guides for in-person groups and online groups are the same. They are not. The guides we get from them need to be adapted for real-time text chats, discussion boards, and sometimes even for video chats.

When a client says that they will take responsibility for writing the guide, respectfully remind them that to internalize the goals and objectives of the project, the moderator should always have a hand in writing the guide. Encourage them to provide you with a "brain dump" of things they'd like to learn from the research, and offer to turn that wish-list into a guide that not only takes advantage of the capabilities of the online platform, but is *in your voice,* so that you can "own" it.

Just as writing an in-person discussion guide requires skill, writing a guide for an online group requires additional skills. As needed remind your clients about this.

• TEXT CHAT •

Tip E-5: Provide Clear Guidelines in Text Chats

Just as at the beginning of in-person focus groups, online moderators should present some tips on how to best be a participant in the discussion. Here's a set of guidelines that has worked well for me over the years. I present the set all at once in a whiteboard at the very beginning of a chat.

1. "Listen" and "talk" to each other—not just to me.
2. Stick to the topic.
3. "STOP!" when asked.
4. Don't worry about spelling or grammar.
5. Don't worry about typing speed.
6. It's OK to disagree, but do it in a nice way.
7. If you get "bumped," just log back in.
8. If I get "bumped," wait for me. I'll be back.
9. Don't multi-task, and minimize distractions.
   (See Tip E-6, for more info.)

It's very important that the list is short and easy to understand. (Feel free to adapt them to make them your own.)

5 | DISCUSSION GUIDES

I typically pick three or four of the guidelines and add some additional commentary. One that I always spend some time on is #6. In addition to what the guideline says, I say in the chat itself, *"Regarding Guideline #6, please treat others in the discussion as you would like to be treated. Feel free to disagree, but do so in a respectful fashion."* Without this guideline, some participants may feel they have the right to denigrate those whose opinions they do not agree with. It's great that participants want to be so open, but even in an anonymous text chat, people's feelings can get hurt. It's best to remind participants to "play nice" with each other.

Taking 1–2 minutes at the beginning of a discussion to present guidelines and highlight a few of them is time well-spent. By doing so, we increase the odds of having compliant and productive participants. That leads to a smooth-running chat, and a good experience for all involved—participants, observers, and the moderator.

• TEXT CHAT •

Tip E-6: Combat Multi-Tasking by Participants in Text Chats

Text chats provide plenty of opportunities for participants to multi-task and lose focus on the online focus group discussion. Without being able to see participants and their environment, it's easy for a text chat participant to peek at texts and emails, carry on a conversation with people around them, shift their attention to a TV program, tend to kids, answer the phone, etc.

When it takes a half-minute or more for one or more participants to answer a simple yes/no question, it's highly likely that the slow-to-respond participants are distracted. And when the moderator calls on a slow-to-respond participant and that participant doesn't respond, it's clear that he or she has temporarily disengaged and is not looking at the screen.

The moderator cannot control these many potential distractions, but they can explicitly ask participants to control them. This is part of giving participants the guidance they need to be good participants. Here's an example of what could be posted at the beginning of every text chat:

"Wherever you may be participating right now (at home, at work, or some other place), please do your best to ignore distractions (phone calls, emails, texts, TV, doorbell, kids, others around you, etc.). When you get distracted, your response time slows down, which means that we may have to go into overtime. So, please stay focused on this online discussion, so we can finish on time. Thanks!"

Of course, this guideline won't eliminate those pesky distractions, but by being open and honest about it up-front, participants are more likely to pay closer attention to the discussion, enabling you to maximize the productivity of your online focus groups.

• TEXT CHAT •

TIP E-7: Right-Size Real-Time Text Chat Discussion Guides

In a text chat, the average question may take 2–3 minutes to be fully answered by all before the group is ready for the next question. Note the use of the word "average" in the preceding sentence. Some questions can be fully answered in as little as 10–15 seconds ("When was the last time you purchased Brand X?"), while other questions might require 3–5 minutes ("What are all of the good things that might be said about Brand Y?").

With this rule of thumb of requiring 2–3 minutes per question, a discussion guide for a 90-minute text chat can be considered full with 30–45 questions, not including follow-up probes seeking clarification or elaboration. Thus, this rule of thumb suggests that a draft of a guide with 100 questions is much too long for a 90-minute group, while one with 20 questions will likely be considerably shorter than 90 minutes.

One more caveat. Keep in mind that each moderator has their own style. And depending on the types of questions being asked, a moderator may be able to ask more or less than 30–45 questions. Use this as a general guideline.

5 | DISCUSSION GUIDES

• TEXT CHAT •

Tip E-8: Narrow the Scope of Questions in Real-Time Text Chats

Let's say that one goal of a project is to collect high-level feedback on a large number of short concepts. One possible approach is that the data collection process could be set up as follows:

1. Present all ideas at the same time.

2. Ask one all-encompassing question: "Which ideas do you most like, and what makes you like each one?"

This approach might work well in an in-person focus group, a video chat, or in an asynchronous discussion board, but it would not work well in a real-time text chat. Why not?

The all-encompassing question deserves a longish, essay-like response. (It's perfect for a discussion board.)

Some will take longer than others to complete their response. Those who finish first are likely to be left "twiddling their thumbs" while waiting for others to finish.

There are likely to be so many different responses that it will be difficult for the moderator, observers, and participants to detect patterns in what the group is saying.

In online text chats, it's best to keep each question very focused/discrete. A better approach would be the following:

- Present all ideas at the same time
- Poll—pick three most preferred ideas from list
- Most preferred idea—likes
- Most preferred idea—dislikes
- 2nd most preferred idea—likes
- 2nd most preferred idea—dislikes

Breaking the process down into smaller chunks makes it easier for everyone, and setting up a structure, starting with the most preferred idea and moving down the list, keeps the discussion highly organized.

This helps participants more easily "digest" what others are saying (which promotes interaction among participants), and it helps the moderator prioritize what probes, if any, should be asked.

The lesson here is that discussion guides for online text chats and online discussion boards can cover the same issues as guides for in-person focus groups and video chats, but they may need to be structured differently to best fit the constraints and advantages of each format.

• TEXT CHAT •

Tip E-9: Get Participants to Answer Multi-Part Questions in a Single Post

In real-time text chats, there are times when asking a multi-part question is appropriate. For example, *"How interesting is this idea?"* and *"What makes you say that?"* But if we ask those two questions separately, it will be cumbersome to identify which answers to the first question go with answers to the second question. Ideally, we'd like to see each participant's answers to both questions **together**.

The questions can be asked by the moderator in a single post, but some participants will see two questions and reflexively answer them separately, in two different posts. That's not helpful. It doesn't help us see their entire thought-process on a multi-part question.

One solution is to make it very clear to participants that they should answer all parts of a question in a single post. Highlight part of the question/instruction to emphasize that we need all answers in a single post. For example, *"In a **SINGLE POST**, tell me two things: 1) how much you're interested in this idea, and 2) a brief explanation about what makes you feel that way."*

It might be wise to purposely ask a question like this early on in the discussion, to give participants some practice in how to answer multi-part questions. Example: *"Before we get started, please tell everyone a bit about yourself. In a **SINGLE POST**, tell us 1) your age, 2) the city/town and state where you live, and 3) the last time you purchased [X]."* One or two participants in a text chat might inadvertently submit three separate posts to answer this three-part question, but when they see the others responding in a single post, they will see how they could have responded.

5 | DISCUSSION GUIDES

• TEXT CHAT •

Tip E-10: Control When Participants See Others' Posts in Real-Time Text Chats

Polling is commonly available on text chat platforms. Polls are a great way to get a quick idea of where the group stands on a question before discussing it in-depth. Typically, the polling function is designed to require participants to respond before they can see others' responses, thereby preventing them from being influenced by how others are voting. This is engaging because it keeps participants in suspense about the results.

Polls are closed-end questions. But what about open-end questions? Some text chat platforms offer this same you-can't-see-others'-posts-until-you-post-your-own feature for open-end questions as well as closed-end questions (polls). This feature can be used on a question-by-question basis. It comes in handy when we want independent responses from everyone to a particular question. Here are some examples of questions that could benefit from "hiding" others' responses from participants until they send their own responses:

"Share three words or phrases that come to mind when you think of food shopping?"

"Approximately how many pairs of shoes are we likely to find in your home?"

"Briefly, what gets you to shop more at Store X than Store Y?"

If available, this option enables moderators to replicate what is commonly done with in-person focus groups, handing out a printed concept and asking participants to jot down answers to a few short questions before having a group discussion about the concept. The writing-down process before discussion encourages them to think on their own and commit to that response at least in the beginning of the question.

If you will be moderating a real-time text chat and want your participants to submit a response to an open-end question before they see others' posts, verify that your platform provider offers this capability.

• TEXT CHAT •

TIP E-11: Schedule Breaks as Needed in Real-Time Chats

Text-based chats and video chats are physically demanding, forcing participants to focus intently on a screen for an extended period of time—typically up to 90 minutes. In rare instances they may be as short as an hour. However, there are times when a session needs to be longer. When a chat is expected to last more than 90 minutes, it's often helpful to take a short break at some time during the session. I suggest around the half-way point. Giving participants two to five minutes to rest their eyes, stretch their fingers, stand up and walk around, or take a quick body break, gives them the energy they need to be fully engaged for the remainder of the session.

Even if a group is less than 90 minutes, a break might be advisable if repetitive tasks are being performed. For example, if the purpose of a discussion is to get feedback on more than 2 concepts, and the same list of diagnostic questions must be asked of each concept, a break will help reduce the fatigue that can set in with repetitive questions.

If moderators plan a break, they should let the group know in advance. That heads-up gives participants something to look forward to.

• TEXT CHAT •

Tip E-12: Offer Tips about Length of Posts in Real-Time Text Chats

An Anecdote. We conducted three real-time text chats with consumers. I was about to launch the next set of three groups—this time with employees. The guide for employees was essentially the same as the guide used for consumers. Because the consumer groups went so well, I expected the same outcome in the employee groups.

The first group of employees had high show rates, and participants had a lot to say about the issues raised. In fact, many responses were quite voluminous, and they were the length of response that I would have expected (and be pleased) to see in an online discussion board. So lengthy were the responses that at the 30-minute mark (of a 90-minute chat) I realized that I was 10 minutes behind. I tried cajoling the group to shorten their posts, which helped a bit, but I continued to fall woefully behind. I asked the observer team to suggest what might be cut from the guide. I followed their suggestions so that the group could end on time.

Before the second employee group happened, we needed to do something to allow us to get through the entire guide. Thinking back, I realized that in the first employee group, the first participants posts were lengthy. My hunch was that the other participants used the first posts they saw as a gauge for how long their own posts should be. Based on that hunch, it appeared that these employees could use some coaching about how long responses should be. In the remaining employee groups, I added the following in my guidelines:

This type of online discussion is designed for quick, gut-level thinking. We have a lot of topics to discuss, so we'll need to move at a fairly quick pace. Here are three quick tips to keep us all on track:

- *Ideally, most of your posts should be no more than 1–2 lines in length. Set that as your goal.*
- *You don't have to post in complete sentences . . . phrases are fine, as long as we understand what you're saying.*
- *If you spend more than 30 seconds (or so) on a post, post it, even if it's not finished. You can always include ". . ." at the end of your post to signal that you will post a continuation of the post.*

Fortunately, I got shorter responses in the subsequent groups, which allowed me to complete the entire guide in the 90 minutes allotted.

The Lesson. Participants appreciate tips on how they should behave— including how long their posts should be. Have the above guideline available if needed to "rein in" the length of posts. Also, consider adding the guideline to the standard list of guidelines you deliver at the beginning of real-time text chats.

• TEXT CHAT | BOARD •

Tip E-13: Strive for Unaided Responses, As Needed

Frequently in qualitative research, we ask some unaided questions that tap into participants' general awareness and general attitudes. These are intended to generate quick, top-of-mind responses. Examples include:

"Which brands of chocolate bars come to mind?"

"What are the names of the hospitals in your area?"

"Give me a list of benefits of putting jigsaw puzzles together."

In online text chats or discussion boards, where we can't see or hear participants, if a participant isn't sure how to answer a question and is uncomfortable appearing to be unknowledgeable, it's easy for them to "cheat" by doing a quick online search or asking someone nearby for help in answering the question. In such cases, a question that was meant to elicit unaided responses results in aided responses.

If unaided responses are the goal in any online text-based discussion, here are ways to make sure those responses are unaided.

- **Tell them what you need.** Explicitly tell your participants that you want top-of-mind answers and explain that they should not look up answers or ask for help from others.

- **Permission to pass.** Give them permission to say, "I don't know." Or tell them that if they draw a blank, it's perfectly fine to simply say so.

- **Must answer to see others' answers.** If the platform allows you to disable their ability to see others' responses until they post their own response, take advantage of this. Let participants know that they will not see others' posts until they post their own response. This is especially helpful in real-time text chats, because a participant or two might be patiently waiting to see others' posts to provide some hints about how to respond, not knowing that they're prevented from seeing others' posts.

- **Emphasize if it's supposed to be a quick exercise.** In the case of discussion boards, emphasize just before asking the question that it's meant to be a quick task, and suggest that they spend no more

5 | DISCUSSION GUIDES

than x number of seconds (20–30?) to respond. This accentuates the need for quick, top-of-mind thoughts.

With the above tactics, online moderators can gather true unaided responses in text-based online qualitative sessions.

• TEXT CHAT | BOARD •

Tip E-14: Be Transparent When Seeking Unbiased Responses

Most real-time text chat platforms and discussion board platforms have a feature that enables researchers to "program" questions and activities such that we get responses from individual participants before they can see others' reactions. It's akin to asking participants in an in-person group to write their answers on a sheet of paper before discussion begins. It helps them commit to an initial answer, but it allows them to change their mind after hearing from others. It produces unbiased responses. Platform providers have different names for this feature; "masked" and "uninfluenced" are popular names.

Here are three suggestions for effective use of insuring unbiased re-actions.

- **Don't use it too frequently.** If participants must constantly answer questions before seeing what others post, they may be turned-off, wondering, "Doesn't the researcher trust me enough to speak for myself?" They may end up ignoring others' posts altogether if they can only see them after they post their own.

- **Let participants know when you need unbiased responses.** Assuming that use of this feature happens only occasionally during a session, it is good to alert participants when it's happening. Otherwise, in the case of real-time text chats, they may be waiting to see what others have to say before posting their own response, which can lead to a lot of wasted time.

- **Explain why independent responses are needed.** Say something like, "I want to see how similar or different everyone's responses are. For that reason, you won't be able to see others' posts until you submit your own response." Or, "It's really important that I get your own response to this question without being influenced by what others say. To make that happen, you'll see others' posts only after you submit your own."

By following these simple guidelines, you'll maximize the effectiveness of the unbiased-response feature in your text-based online focus groups.

Note that while concerns about insuring unbiased responses are not as great in video chats, it's still useful to inform participants of your rationale for such responses.

• TEXT CHAT | BOARD •

Tip E-15: Use Text Formatting and Layout Options to Help Communicate

When we prepare discussion guides for in-person focus groups, we typically use a single font, with few, if any, visual enhancements. When we use that guide during the group, we will naturally put emphasis on certain words or phrases when we deliver questions aloud, to be clear about what we are asking.

But when we post a question in an online text chat or discussion board, the nuances of speech are absent. To put emphasis where it needs to go, take advantage of font options (e.g., **bolding**, CAPS, *italics*, underlining, color, and font size); or make creative use of spacing.

Here's an example related to real-time chats.

One Way to Show the Question	A Better Way to Show the Question
"How might you benefit from this idea?"	"How might you **BENEFIT** from this idea?"

In this case, the keyword "benefit" jumps out from the screen because it is capitalized and bolded. Participants quickly get the gist of the question from that one word. That enables them to focus their attention and begin composing a response.

Here's an example related to asynchronous discussion boards.

One Way to Show the Question	A Better Way to Show the Question
"Tell us the story of the last time you brought your vehicle in for servicing. What did you like about the experience? What did you dislike about it? If you could have changed just one thing about that experience, what would it have been, and how would you have benefited from that change?"	Tell us the story of the last time you brought your vehicle in for servicing. 1. What did you **LIKE** about the experience? 2. What did you **DISLIKE** about it? 3. If you could have **CHANGED ONE THING** about that experience, what would it have been, **AND** *how would you have benefited from that change?*

Notice several things about the "better" version:

- The verbiage is exactly the same in both versions.
- Using bullet points makes it clear that there are three things to do.
- The use of bold highlights the focus of each sub-question.
- Using italics in the last bullet accentuates the need for further explanation.

Using font options and spacing tactics can help participants quickly understand questions. This helps them give complete answers and can reduce the need for follow-up probes.

• TEXT CHAT | BOARD •

Tip E-16: Know the Pros and Cons of Discussion Guide Uploading Options

A standard practice in qualitative research (in-person or online) is for discussion guides to be developed by the moderator in collaboration with the project team. The guide is almost always in Word, and it typically goes through several versions before it is finalized. In online text-based studies, after the guide is approved, it, along with any stimulus materials, will need to be uploaded to the text chat or discussion board platform. There are different ways to get the guide uploaded.

- **Manually upload from Word.** The most prevalent method is the do-it-yourself approach, copying and pasting online discussion guides from a Word document to the platform. This can take anywhere from 30–60 minutes. The moderator might do this, but if an assistant is available, they can do this as well.

- **Automatically upload from Excel.** Some text-based platforms enable automatic uploads of guides from Excel files. The Excel files must conform to the platform provider's spreadsheet template.
- **Platform provider uploads for you.** Some platform providers may offer to upload the guide (in Word) for you. If they do, the service may be free, or there may be a modest fee.

There are advantages and disadvantages for each of the three options.

Upload Method	Advantages	Disadvantages
Manually, from Word	• Forces another look at the guide, resulting in tweaks that improve the guide	• Labor intensive, tedious process • Time-consuming
Automatically, from Excel	• No need for a third party • Fast • No tedious cutting and pasting	• Guide in Excel may seem "odd" to client team • May require extra step to convert the guide from Word to Excel
Platform Provider Uploads for You	• Fantastic if it's free • Less time "wasted" on administrative tasks	• May add cost to the project • May still require time to double-check that the upload was done accurately

More on manual uploads

When I manually upload guides, I almost always find ways to improve them. The manual process forces me to scrutinize each question one more time. Invariably, I find ways to tweak questions. I might realize that a question can be worded better, that a short preface to a question would be helpful, that adding a new question before asking another would serve as a good transition, etc. If I automatically upload the guide

5 | DISCUSSION GUIDES

or if somebody takes care of uploading the guide for me, those opportunities for improvements are less likely to be realized.

You might consider my desire to manually upload a guide to border on obsessive-compulsiveness. (If so, maybe you're right!) But it's important to remember that in text-based online qual, it's very important to get questions worded as perfectly as possible. It's easy in an in-person group to re-phrase a poorly worded question without losing much time, but in a text-based environment (both real-time chats and discussion boards), having to clarify questions takes valuable time. That's why discussion guides in text-based online methods require a lot more attention to detail than guides for in-person groups or video chats.

While manually uploading a guide seems mundane, it can serve as an additional quality control check in the process. That extra layer of quality control has three benefits: 1) the group will run more efficiently, 2) participants will have a better experience and be more engaged, and 3) insights will more readily emerge.

· BOARD ·

TIP E-17: Manage Discussion Board Participant Expectations When a Board Launches

Online discussion boards are still new to many people, so recruits need to be coached about what to expect. Tip D-2 suggests what to tell potential respondents about the discussion board experience while they are being recruited—before they agree to participate. This tip focuses on what discussion board recruits should be told when the board begins. These points can be made in the instruction email that accompanies their login instructions, in the moderator's welcome message at the beginning of the board, or both.

- **General Orientation.** Remind participants of what they were told during recruitment: the number of days the board will be open, their daily time commitment, when they should visit each day, and the requirement to participate fully on all days to earn the incentive.
- **Follow-up Questions.** Inform them that you (the moderator) will be reading all responses and will likely ask follow-up questions if a

post is incomplete, unclear, or sparks another follow-up question from the moderator. Stress that all follow-up questions must be answered to earn their incentive.

- **Interaction.** Emphasize the importance of interaction with other respondents. Consider challenging them to respond to a minimum number (for example, two) of other participants' posts each day, to stimulate interaction.
- **Technical Issues.** Assure them that tech support is available for any problems or issues that may arise. Provide them with contact info for that support.
- **Other Issues.** Tell them to inform you if anything gets in the way of their participation.

It is important to remind participants of your expectations of them at the very beginning of the board, so there are no surprises or misinterpretations.

· BOARD ·

Tip E-18: Include Guidelines in Online Discussion Board Introductions

When they agree to participate in a multi-day online discussion board, participants should be told what to expect, and what's expected of them. Later, when reminder notices are sent and login instructions are issued, those expectations should be stated again, to minimize any surprises once the board launches. Expectations should be shared one more time at the beginning of the discussion board itself.

There's no need to rush through the introduction in a discussion board because the clock is not ticking like it is in real-time chats. Discussion boards are more relaxed. The moderator's introduction should include most (if not all) of the following:

- The discussion topic
- Study sponsor (if appropriate)
- Disclosures about confidentiality and the presence of observers
- How long the board will be open (and whether any break days are planned)

5 | DISCUSSION GUIDES

- When new questions are typically posted
- Average amount of time they should expect to spend at the board each day
- How often they should visit the board each day
- Whether it's a group discussion or a one-on-one interview
- If it's a group discussion, specify whether and how often they should interact with each other
- Whether they need to respond to follow-up questions
- How to find follow-up questions
- Requirements to earn the incentive
- Tips on keeping up with the discussion

These guidelines should be delivered in a friendly, matter-of-fact tone. They should be written as the moderator speaks so that they come across as coming from a human being. Some or all of the introductory info could be delivered via video to which the moderator provides a link.

Consider asking participants to acknowledge that they have read and understand the background and guidelines. Even better—if the platform enables it—prevent participants from accessing the first question unless they give you the acknowledgment you are looking for. This is more likely to get participants to carefully read your introductory remarks.

It's important to be transparent to our participants at all times about what they need to do to be a "good" participant. Sharing this information multiple times strengthens that transparency.

• BOARD •

Tip E-19: Be Respectful of Discussion Board Participants' Time

Unlike in-person focus groups and real-time online focus groups (text chats and video chats), asynchronous discussion boards typically last days. This length of time can potentially make moderators and observers feel that participants are at our beck and call for days instead of hours, giving us the freedom to ask more follow-ups than we have time to ask in other types of focus groups.

Remember, though, that participants have been told how much time they should expect to spend each day on board activities. Typically, we tell them to expect to spend an average of 30–45 minutes each day on discussion board activities. If we repeatedly require them to put in substantially more time than we told them, they can justifiably become irritated. They may feel taken advantage of. In extreme cases, they might leave the discussion, even at the risk of losing their incentive, because it's requiring more time than they expected.

Thus, it's important to be realistic in terms of how much time it will take participants to fulfill their role. Here are some ways to keep participant work-loads in line with their expectations.

- **Control the number of participants.** In interactive discussion boards, having more participants in the group means more time will be needed to read and react to others' posts. To foster interaction, keep the number of participants to 12–16.

- **Don't include too many questions in the guide.** With fewer questions, they will spend more time on each one, and they will be more willing to read others' posts and interact with their fellow participants. (See also Tip E-20.)

- **Ask clear questions.** Ambiguously worded questions will lead to less useful posts, forcing the moderator to ask clarifying follow-ups that demand more time of participants. Invest plenty of time up-front crafting the discussion guide.

- **Don't inundate participants with too many follow-ups.** The only exception to this is when participants are "sloppy" with unclear or incomplete responses. If they were properly informed of the need for clear and complete answers, it is reasonable for them to expect us to remind them of the need to comply.

- **Manage client expectations about further probing.** They need to know that we may not be able to ask every additional follow-up question they would like to have asked. While it's tempting to ask "just one more question," it's important to distinguish between nice-to-know and need-to-know extra information.

- **Keep a placeholder in the guide for extra questions on the last day.** Keep the workload light on the last day, reserving space for any

5 | DISCUSSION GUIDES

questions/issues that come up that the team hadn't anticipated. (See also Tip E-32.)

- **Consider follow-up work.** Ask some (or all) participants to answer some additional questions for an extra incentive. This can be another discussion board, a phone interview/video chat, or even an email exchange. It's a way to gain additional insights more economically than running a new study.

· B O A R D ·

TIP E-20: Right-Size Discussion Board Moderator's Guides

The length of discussion guides for discussion boards will vary depending on many factors.

Factors Impacting Guide Length	Example
The amount of time participants should be active on the board each day.	The less time participants are told to spend on the board, the fewer questions there should be in the guide.
The mix of questions requiring short vs. long answers.	If most questions will require long answers, there should be fewer questions in the guide.
Whether stimuli are included in the guide.	Showing stimuli in the guide—which is a good practice—will naturally lengthen the guide.
Whether the board is being used for IDIs (one-on-one interviews), an interactive group discussion, or a combination of both.	If participants don't need to read and react to other participants' posts, they have more time to answer questions, so the guide can theoretically be longer.

Guides for discussion boards are typically longer (more words) than those created for any other type of guide (in-person or online). This is because every extra comment from the moderator that might otherwise be ad-libbed in a real-time setting should be included in a discussion board guide. Why? To make the moderator seem more human, more casual, less rigid/robotic. The language used in a discussion board guide can be more like the moderator actually speaks.

Number of Questions in a Guide

Another way to think about the appropriate length of a discussion board discussion guide is to offer some best-practices for the number of questions that might reasonably fit in a day's worth of discussion board activity.

- **Interactive group discussions.** Assuming 45 minutes of work per day, 12–16 participants, a fully interactive discussion (i.e., participants see each other's posts), and a good mix of questions eliciting short vs. long answers, a general rule of thumb for guide length is 5–10 questions per day.

  As mentioned in Tip E-9, questions may be grouped into sets. Sets typically consist of 2–5 questions that meaningfully go together. Each question in a set will ideally require short answers (1–2 sentences), but could include a question or two that will elicit longer answers.

  Remember that the fewer questions there are in a day, the more time participants will have to give fuller responses plus read others' posts and interact with them. Why? Because if we tell them to expect to spend 45 minutes per day on the board and they answer all of the moderator's questions in 20–25 minutes, they still have budgeted time to interact with other participants. *("Oh. It took less time to answer the questions than I thought. They told me to spend around 45 minutes. I'm all caught up, so I may as well look to see what others are saying.")*

- **IDIs.** If we are using an online discussion board for one-on-ones instead of a group discussion, we can ask more questions because participants don't have to spend any time reading and reacting to others' posts. All of their time can be devoted to composing responses to the moderator's questions. In this case, 10–15 questions per day would be a good rule-of-thumb (assuming that we've told them to expect to spend around 45 minutes each day, and that the questions will elicit a mix of short and long answers).

5 | DISCUSSION GUIDES

· BOARD ·

TIP E-21: Spread the Work Evenly

When we recruit for a discussion board, we always tell participants to expect to spend a certain amount of time on the board each day. Our general rule of thumb is to suggest 30–45 minutes per day. We commit to not keep our participants longer than that amount of time, unless, of course, they're really engaged and want to stay longer.

If we tell participants to expect to spend x amount of time at the board each day, and they actually complete their "work" within that amount of time, they are happy and very likely to return on subsequent days. They see that we respect them by providing fairly accurate estimate of how much effort we require of them.

If participants end up putting a lot more time into the board than they expected, we risk losing them, especially on the first day of a discussion board. If they have the impression that we intentionally misrepresented the scope of work involved, they might be fed up with us and simply not return. In such cases, attrition rates can rise, and recruitment costs may go up.

To keep this attrition to a minimum, we spread the questions as evenly as possible over the days the board is running. Most of the time, this is easy to do. But sometimes it's impossible to keep the work load even. For example, in a concept evaluation study, it might be important to have all concepts evaluated in a single day, perhaps requiring 45–60 minutes of participant time, rather than 30–45. When this happens, we do the following:

- Inform participants early on of the unevenness of the workload. Explain why it's uneven.
- Make the workload lighter on another day, to "balance" the effort required.
- Assure them that the total amount of time they will end up spending will be in line with what they were told during recruitment.

It's all about being transparent with our participants, managing their expectations, and treating them with respect.

90 MR. ONLINE'S PLAYBOOK

• BOARD •

TIP E-22: Give Titles to Discussion Board Topics and Questions/Activities

If the discussion board platform you are using allows you to customize titles for topics, questions, or activities, take advantage of that feature. Titles act as a table of contents or a road map for the discussion. They offer a preview of what the discussion will be about. Good titles not only inform participants and observers, but they can also intrigue, entertain, and motivate users to engage in the process.

Topics. Let's say that we're doing a project for a smartphone manufacturer. The company wants reactions to two possible new smartphone concepts. A 3-day discussion board will be used. The discussion guide has been approved, and it's time to upload the guide to the discussion board platform. Shown in the table below are two options for presenting the topics.

List of Discussion Board Topics: Option A	List of Discussion Board Topics: Option B
• Introduction	• Introduction
• DAY 1—Topic A	• Storytelling: Favorite Phone Features
• DAY 1—Topic B	• Smart Phone Brand Reviews
• DAY 2—Topic C	• Future Smartphone "Wish List"
• DAY 2—Topic D	• Evaluate Concept R
• DAY 3—Topic E	• Evaluate Concept S
• DAY 3—Topic F	• Taking it a Step Further
• Wrap-Up	• Wrap-Up

While both are serviceable approaches to titling topics, it should be obvious that Option B is more informative and transparent. Option A, on the other hand, comes across as unnecessarily secretive and unengaging.

Questions

Take the smartphone concept study a step further, and focus on questions that might be asked in the "Smartphone Brand Reviews" topic, the third topic in the above list. As with topic titles, question titles give

5 | DISCUSSION GUIDES

participants a sense of the direction the discussion will take. But care must be taken in not providing information in titles that could bias responses. Compare the three sets of options in the table below.

Smartphone Brand Reviews—Possible Questions		
Weak Titles	**Better Titles**	**Strongest Titles**
• Question 3.1	• Brands That Come to Mind	• Brands That Come to Mind
• Question 3.2	• Your Favorite Brand	• Your Favorite Brand
• Question 3.3	• Perceptions of Apple	• Perceptions of Brand X
• Question 3.4	• Perceptions of Samsung	• Perceptions of Brand Y
• Question 3.5	• Perceptions of LG	• Perceptions of Brand Z

With Option A, the participant would see that there are five questions in this topic. The "3" in all five question numbers signifies that it's the third topic. Relying on question numbers alone does not make for an engaging or informative set of questions.

Option B is an improvement over Option A, but some titles share too much information, naming brands that could be included when responding to the brand awareness question. We will NOT get an accurate read on unaided awareness with this set of question titles.

Option C is best. Unlike Option B, specific brand names aren't included in any question titles, allowing us to get a true read on unaided brand awareness.

Another benefit of good titles

Beyond being informative and transparent, good topic and question titles are helpful in another way. Let's say that a participant wants to amend their response they posted yesterday. If they have an easy way of finding where their original response was, they are more likely to post that amendment. If they have difficulty finding the post (as is more likely to be the case in the purely-numbered titling scheme, they may forego sharing that extra bit of insight.

The bottom line of this tip is to remember to take the time to come up with topic and question titles that will entice your participants and help them navigate back and forth in the discussion.

• VIDEO | TEXT CHAT | BOARD •

Tip E-23: Use Question Sets in Discussion Boards

One of the advantages of discussion boards is that we can ask many questions at once—as a question set. From the participant's perspective, answering a question set is like answering a multi-part essay question. Participants are provided direction in terms of what points need to be addressed in their responses.

Here are some examples.

- **Concept Evaluations.** A single post from a participant could include: 1) an overall reaction, 2) a list of likes and dislikes, 3) a rating of how unique the concept is, 4) questions the participant has that the concept doesn't answer, and 5) what might make the concept more appealing. Seeing answers from a participant to all of these components provides us with a holistic view of how they perceive the concept. It helps the moderator to see and probe on any inconsistencies in responses in the question set.

- **Storytelling.** When asking about a recent experience with a product or service, ask participants to tell the story as they would to a friend, and highlight what the story should include (when it happened, what prompted the usage occasion, who else was present at the time, how satisfactory the experience was, what would have made it better, etc.).

- **Projective Exercises.** When showing an array of stimuli (words, images, colors, etc.) as part of a projective exercise about what stimuli best match a brand or resonate with them on a particular topic, don't ask two different questions—which ones best fit the brand and which ones are the poorest fit. Ask both questions in one question set.

If the researcher requires responses to all questions in the set, number each question and ask participants to use those numbers in their responses. Using the numbers helps participants keep track of what parts of the question set they have or have not answered, and it helps the

5 | DISCUSSION GUIDES   93

moderator quickly assess whether the participant has responded to all elements in the question set.

Question sets will typically require more time for the participant to respond. Thus, it's best to not ask question set after question set, otherwise the tasks will grow tiresome. Vary things a bit by asking an easy/short-response question after a question set; doing so will keep participants "on their toes," not knowing what type of question will come up next.

• BOARD •

Tip E-24: Specify How Much Depth Is Needed in Discussion Board Responses

Many online discussion board participants are first-timers. They may already be familiar with online quantitative surveys and not understand the difference between qualitative and quantitative research, so when they agree to participate in a discussion board, they might incorrectly presume that it will be very much like quant surveys. As such, they may think that short answers to open-ended questions are all that's needed.

More often than not, though, we need more than a few words, or even more than one or two sentences to some responses. Thus, it's best to provide guidance about how much depth you are looking for in response to certain questions. Here are some ways to accomplish this:

- **Provide timing guidelines.** Specify how much time they should spend in replying to the question. Examples:
  - ○ "This shouldn't take long. Please spend no more than two minutes on this."
  - ○ "This is a really important question today, and I need as much detail as possible. Please spend at least 2–3 minutes on this."
- **Like a conversation.** Ask them to respond as if they are talking to a friend, or replying to a close friend's email or text.
- **Tell a story.** Ask them to respond in story form, with a post that has a beginning, middle, and end, containing all of the necessary details that will not leave the reader with any unanswered questions.
- **Use examples.** If there's a prior question that generated the amount

of depth you're looking for, point out "good posts" for participants to use as a benchmark about depth.

By giving clear direction about the depth of response required, participants will be more confident about their responses, and they have a more satisfying participant experience because they receive fewer follow-ups from the moderator asking for more detail. In addition, you will be happier because you'll spend less time "nagging" participants for more depth.

· BOARD ·

TIP E-25: Use Masked/Uninfluenced Mode Sparingly

One feature of most online discussion board platforms is giving the moderator control over whether and when participants see others' responses to a question. There are typically three options. The names of these options vary from platform to platform, but the idea is the same. Here are the three:

- **Regular**—Upon opening a question, participants see all responses that have been already posted.
- **Masked/Uninfluenced**—The participant sees others' posts only after posting their own response.
- **Interview**—The participant never sees others' posts to that question.

The moderator is typically able to choose which option to use on a question-by-question basis.

Even online, there is the possibility for "group think" to happen. Thus, the Masked/Uninfluenced option is handy when we want to be absolutely certain that participants are giving us their independent views (for example, first reaction to a concept) without being influenced by what anybody else in the group says.

It's tempting to ask every question in Masked/Uninfluenced mode, but be cautious about over-using it. If the Uninfluenced option is used too much, it may give participants the impression that we don't trust them to speak their own minds. And if they begin feeling that way, their willingness to interact with others might diminish.

Thus, use the Masked/Uninfluenced option when absolutely necessary. Additionally, announce to participants when it's in use, and explain why you are doing this. For example, you might say, *"I want to see all the different ways panelists think about X. To accomplish that, I've set this question up so that you won't see others' posts until you post your own."* It's straight-forward and transparent.

• BOARD •

Tip E-26: Allow Discussion Board Participants to Interact with Each Other

Many online moderators use discussion boards almost exclusively for IDIs. This is especially appropriate . . .

- When we don't want respondents to be influenced by what others have to say.
- When there are so many questions to ask that we doubt there would be any extra time for participants to interact with each other.

That said, participants enjoy reading others' posts. They like to see how their views compare to others. Seeing others' posts could spark additional thoughts/ideas which otherwise might not occur.

Most discussion-board platforms give moderators the option of controlling—on a question-by-question or activity-by-activity basis—whether and when a participant can see others' responses. This provides maximum flexibility for the moderator. If you tend to not have participants interact with each other in discussion boards, think about taking advantage of opportunities to do so. Here are some ways to include some participant interactivity into discussion boards.

- **Concept Tests.** On Day 1, keep things interactive through the warm-up. Let participants get to know each other. Once it's time to get reactions to concepts, wall participants off from one another. Tell them that after they evaluate all concepts, they will "see" each other again. Thus, allow them to get to know one another a bit, have them do their concept evaluations independently of one another, then bring them back together to discuss other issues as a group.
- **Sensitive Subjects.** Text-based online methods maximize anonym-

96 MR. ONLINE'S PLAYBOOK

ity, making participants feel more comfortable sharing their opinions and experiences—especially on sensitive topics. On sensitive topics that they otherwise don't talk to others about, they might actually appreciate the opportunity to share their thoughts and feelings with others like themselves, and see what others have to say.

- **"Just for Fun."** If there is any "free time" available, consider adding interactive questions/activities. Let participants know up front that there will be a mix of private and public responses. The variety of activities makes the process more engaging for them.

So, take advantage of opportunities to have participants chat with each other in online discussion boards. It can make the user experience more engaging, and it has the potential of producing additional insights.

· BOARD ·

Tip E-27: Use This Checklist to Maximize Participant Interaction in Discussion Boards

Getting participants to interact with each other in a discussion board is one of the biggest challenges an online moderator will face. A sequential series of tactics is usually needed get desired levels of interaction.

STEP 1: Be Clear About Your Expectations

- When recruiting participants, make sure they know that interaction is expected—"talking" to each other and not just answering the moderator's questions.
- When login instructions are sent, remind them of the need to interact with each other.
- The moderator's introductory remarks at the beginning of the board should include a reminder of the need to interact.
- Any reminders notices could also include encouraging words to interact.
- Be clear that incentives will be paid only to those who answer all main questions and all follow-up questions—whether those follow-ups come from the moderator or other participants. See Tip G-30.

5 | DISCUSSION GUIDES

STEP 2: Give Specific Examples of How They Can Interact

- Permit participants to ask questions of other participants.
- Encourage them to respond to somebody's post if they strongly agree or disagree (in whole or in part) with a post.
- Allow them to build on others' posts/ideas.
- If the platform used includes emoticons (e.g., like, dislike, etc.), point out that they are available to easily let others know what they think about others' posts.

STEP 3: Make it Easy/Fun for Participants to Interact

- If the platform gives the option of using like/dislike/etc. "stickers" (as on Facebook and Instagram), be sure to enable them.
- Make a game of it. Challenge participants to post a response to at least x number (usually 2–3) others' posts each day, and remind them of this as needed.
- Publicly applaud the first participants who interact with others.
- Consider paying a "bonus" incentive to those who interact with others at some minimal level.
- Ask follow-up questions that require participants to review others' posts to respond; this is designed to get them in the habit (if they're not already doing so) of reading and reacting to others' posts.

Use the above checklist to maximize interaction levels among participants in discussion boards.

· BOARD ·

Tip E-28: Require Interaction in Online Discussion Boards, As Needed

Tip E-27 suggests that to foster interaction among participants in discussion boards, moderators should challenge participants to post a response to at least 2–3 others' posts each day, and to remind them of this challenge daily. The rationale behind this suggestion is that by setting a low bar of interaction with other participants, they'll see how easy it is and interact more than the minimum level requested.

This form of encouragement helps, but it doesn't guarantee across-the-board interaction among discussion-board participants. If, for whatever reason, the research firm feels that interaction among participants is imperative, it may consider **requiring** a minimum level of interaction. In this case, participants should be told during recruitment, and with reminders as needed while the board is live that they **must** *interact with at least x number of other participants each day to earn their incentive.*

The project team can decide whether to withhold all or part of the incentive for participants who do not comply with this order. In all fairness, participants who don't interact with others at all should receive most of the promised incentive if they at least answer all moderator questions. But the decision about whether and how much to withhold is up to the study team.

· BOARD ·

Tip E-29: Prevent Discussion Board Participants from Skipping Questions

The default setting on most discussion boards allows participants to see and read all launched questions before answering them. This gives them the opportunity to answer the questions in any order they wish, and it allows them to skip questions. The advantage of this is that it puts participants in control and gives them maximum flexibility. Theoretically, it enhances the user experience. From a research perspective, however, this can be dangerous. Here are two examples:

- We typically want to hear about unaided awareness of brands BEFORE we ask about the pros and cons of particular brands.
- We typically want to discuss problems with a type of product or service and perhaps allow participants to brainstorm about desired solutions BEFORE exposing participants to new concepts.

Think of the permission to see all questions beforehand as being like an open-book test in school. In some instances that may be appropriate given the project's information objectives, but most of the time we need to introduce topics and questions in a particular order.

Fortunately, most (if not all) discussion board platforms give the moderator the option of forcing participants to answer questions in a particular order. Taking advantage of that option assures that participants will answer all questions in a set order and makes sure they don't skip any questions along the way.

There are several advantages to having participants see and answer questions in a pre-set order.

- Participants won't jump ahead to a question or topic that we don't yet want them to see.
- If participants forget where they left off, they won't accidentally skip any questions that they thought they had answered.

If a platform's default allows questions to be answered in any order the participant desires, you should not accept that default and take advantage of options that guide participants along a path of seeing and answering questions in the order you want.

· BOARD ·

Tip E-30: Set the Bar High to Go Deeper

Within a discussion board, we typically give participants a relatively quick and easy task to warm them up to a new topic. Creating lists is a quick and easy task. Examples of list-type questions appear on the left side of the table below.

One Way to Ask for a List	Better Way to Ask for a List
Tell me what you like about this new idea?	Regardless of your level of interest in this idea, list FIVE things you like about it.
What are potential uses of this product/service?	Give me at least THREE potential uses of this product/service.
What are some benefits of using public transportation?	Give me SEVEN potential benefits of using public transportation.

Whether using a discussion board for a group discussion or IDIs, participants may give one or two very short (top-of-mind) answers to questions on the left side of the above table. Challenge participants to dig deeper by specifying the number of items you want to see on their lists, as shown on the right side of the table.

In discussion boards used for group discussions, set up the listing question so that participants can't see others' posts until they post their own. This will force individuals to come up with their own lists, preventing them from copying what others have posted.

The key is to set the number of items in the list to a reasonable number (more than one or two, but not 20 or 30!). If participants can't reach the number of items you ask for, they'll simply say, "I can't think of any more," and move on. Thus, it's okay to set the bar a bit high, but not too high.

If this is truly meant to be a quick activity, the question can be amended with an instruction similar to this one: *"Work quickly, and don't think too much about it. Give yourself ONE minute to come up with as many answers to this question as you can."* That will give them a clear time-limit to work with, keeping them from spending too much time on it, and saving them time to spend on other questions.

• VIDEO | BOARD •

TIP E-31: Take Advantage of Video Capabilities of Discussion Board Platforms

By their nature, discussion board platforms are text-based. That said, some platforms make it easy for participants to record and upload videos to the platform. Most researchers will readily admit that including well-curated video clips can enhance the quality and impact of the report, yet putting together video reels for reports can be time-consuming.

By carefully crafting a lean video capture program, researchers can provide value-add videos to their reports without too much additional effort. How? Here are some easy ways to accomplish this:

- **Ask for video posts at the end of the board.** Don't worry about capturing videos for every topic or activity in the discussion. Think about a capstone question at the end of the discussion that would lend itself to being included in the Executive Summary or at the end of the Detailed Findings section of a report.
- **Plant the seed.** Once recruited, inform participants that they MAY be asked to record one or two videos at the end of the interview

or discussion. Stress that videos will be optional. This foreshadowing at the beginning of the discussion will make it easier for them to say "yes" if and when they are invited to post a video.

- **Be selective.** There's no need to ask everyone to submit videos. You only need a few good video clips to enhance your reports. Don't invite anyone to submit videos unless they seem to be good communicators.
- **Offer an additional incentive.** This task requires extra work for participants. As such, they deserve to be fairly compensated. Budget for this beforehand.
- **Ask for only a small number of videos**. It'll be less work for participants, and less work for those who will be culling clips or creating a highlight reel.
- **Keep video tasks tightly focused.** Set boundaries for participants. Tell them that the videos should be no more than a certain length (e.g., half a minute, 1–2 minutes). With less video to review, the editing process will go faster.

Thus, in keeping the number of video questions to a minimum, by asking only the "best" participants to record videos, by making the opportunity optional, by offering an additional incentive, and by coaching invitees to create short videos, the amount of time needed to create clips or reels will be reduced. And your report will shine.

· BOARD ·

Tip E-32: Leave Room for Extra Questions on the Last Day of a Discussion Board

Oftentimes, the insights gained in the course of an online discussion board lead to additional questions that we'd like to ask our participants before the board closes. But if the guide is already full, and we know our participants are putting in at least as much time as we told them to expect to spend in participating, then it may be unfair to ask any additional questions. Here are three ways to get those extra questions to fit.

- **Pre-Reserve Space in the Guide.** When developing the guide, leave space for 2–3 additional questions/issues to be asked on the last day. The guide will appear to be "lighter" on the last day compared to the prior days. The team can decide which (if any) extra questions should be asked before the last day.

- **Replace Less Important Questions if Needed.** If the information objectives require a full guide with no room for any additional unanticipated questions on the last day, identify 1–2 questions which might be eliminated if more critical questions arise. If no critical questions emerge before the last day, the guide stays as is. If more important questions emerge, then it should be easy to fit them in since questions that might be eliminated were already identified.

- **Make Extra Questions Optional.** Let's say the guide is full and there are no questions that are considered expendable. If critical additional questions emerge before the last day, go ahead and add them, but make them optional. Everyone may not answer them, but if the discussion topic is engaging, if the additional questions are intriguing, and if a heartfelt plea is made to answer them (without penalty if they are not answered), then at least some insights will be gleaned. Consider offering an additional "bonus" incentive for those who answer these extra questions.

Of course, another option is to conduct another discussion board at a later date. Once the analysis is complete from the first board, even more questions might arise, making an additional discussion board worthwhile. To save on recruitment, consider inviting those who participated in the original boards. This extra board does not need to be as long as the original ones.

· VIDEO ·

Tip E-33: Beware of Backgrounds in Video Chat Platforms

Many video chat platforms enable participants to either blur their actual background, or choose a virtual background. This capability is valuable because it allows participants to show something about themselves (their interests) to the group.

But there's a downside. Sometimes we want to have participants show

5 | DISCUSSION GUIDES   103

us something in the course of a discussion. Here are some examples:

- As part of "homework" to get them thinking about a product category, we ask them to bring a favored household item to show-and-tell to the group.
- To prepare for a story-telling exercise, we ask them to bring a photo that highlights something they really enjoyed about a previous vacation.
- To gather uninfluenced responses to a stimulus presented during a focus group, we ask them to jot down some initial impressions on a sheet of paper to later show the entire group.

However, when the blurred or special backgrounds are used in video chats, the webcam has a much shallower depth of field; if what is shown is too far away from the participant's face, the item they are showing will not be in focus.

If it's important to have participants show things in a video chat, you may need to ask participants to turn off those special backgrounds. This will take time during the group to make sure this happens, and may or may not be worth the extra time required.

Thus, it's important to think through in advance whether you'll want them to show a physical object to the group, then either have them turn off their blurred/alternate background (remember, not all consumers know how to do this) or come up with an alternate way of having them share those visuals with the group. Two alternatives are:

- Use the chat feature to share first reactions to stimuli, asking them to hold off on posting their text until AFTER you ask them to send.
- Have them take a photo of what it is you'd like them to show-and-tell, then have each participant take turns sharing their screen to show that photo.

SECTION 6

Observer Management

Let's not forget the observers! The experience for them will be different than it is for in-person groups. Also, in online platforms, all observers have access to the moderator, giving them free rein to ask additional questions. This needs to be controlled. The tips in this section should help.

• TEXT CHAT •

Tip F-1: Control Observer Requests During Real-Time Chats

In real-time text chats or video chats, all observers have the ability to send messages to the moderator, requesting additional probes. This is the digital equivalent of sending notes from the back room during in-person groups. Getting too many interruptions from observers can be distracting for the online moderator. In addition, if the moderator honors all observers' requests, the discussion may lengthen to the point that critical topics in the guide may need to be glossed over or eliminated altogether.

One way to keep observer requests to a manageable number is to designate a single observer as the one to send messages to the moderator. All observers can suggest additional probes, but the designated observer will prioritize these additional requests and forward them to the moderator. Be sure that all observers are informed who the designee is, so that they will not be upset if the moderator does not ask their suggested additional questions.

This approach is similar to a tactic that's often used by moderators of in-person groups. When the moderator takes a scheduled break to meet with observers in the back room to collect additional questions to be asked, it's more efficient when the moderator is directed by one observer in the back room. That person should be cognizant of how much

6 | OBSERVER MANAGEMENT 105

time will be available for any additional questions, and should be fully informed of the study objectives so that only those questions that support the objectives get asked.

· TEXT CHAT ·

Tip F-2: Make the Real-Time Text Chat Observation Process Engaging

Before COVID, we encouraged client teams to observe online focus groups (real-time text chats and real-time video chats) and to meet in one place to observe the sessions, despite the fact that participants were remote. The benefit of meeting in-person is the community spirit that helps the observing group focus on what participants are saying.

Since COVID, more and more client groups are relying on remote viewing of focus groups, even of in-person focus groups.

There are still ways to keep the communal experience alive and make the observation process more engaging, enjoyable, and productive. Here are some examples:

- **Make it fun.** Send an Observer's Kit to each Observer. The kit can include snacks (don't forget the M&Ms!), a bottle of water, and a simple worksheet (one copy for each session) that encourages them to take notes (e.g., new news, confirmed news, possible changes to the guide). A "deluxe" kit can also include a voucher or coupon for meal delivery. (NOTE: The savings on travel can support the expense of these packages.)

- **Give observers a way to *talk*.** Include an open phone line for observers to dial in during each session. This can stimulate some off-the-cuff thinking and will supplement the chat function that's likely already available on the platform.

- **Maintain debrief calls.** Schedule a debrief call at the end of each day to collect everyone's input on what they observed that day and to reach consensus on any needed process changes for subsequent groups.

As more and more organizations entice workers to come into the office at least occasionally, observing online focus groups in-person becomes more of a possibility. If a large-screen video display is available in a conference room for everyone to look at, it can simulate looking through a one-way mirror at a brick-and-mortar focus group facility. Otherwise, everyone can observe via their own laptops, but still be physically present with each other.

These enhancements to the observer experience could help get more team members engaged in observing (together in-person or remotely) real-time online focus groups—and getting the most out of those groups.

• BOARD •

Tip F-3: Strengthen the Online Discussion Board Observation Experience

Perhaps one of the biggest challenges with online discussion boards is getting observers to actually observe. There are several things that can be done to increase the chances that observers will actually observe. Here are some options:

- **Block Time.** Direct each member of the observer team to actually block time on their calendars for board observation. That time should be sacred. If it's not blocked, other things in their workday will inevitably encroach on their observation time.

- **Divide and Conquer (Part A).** If multiple boards in a project are happening at once, divide the team up so that an equal number of observers is assigned to each board. This lightens the burden for each individual observer.

- **Divide and Conquer (Part B).** If there are many observers, assign particular participants for them to follow. This could be a random assignment, or something more meaningful (e.g., some observe older or younger participants, or male vs. female participants). This should help make their observation duties more manageable.

- **Quote of the Day.** Ask each observer to nominate one respondent's post that resonated with them (for any reason) that day. They can do this by simply adding a comment in the board to the notable

6 | OBSERVER MANAGEMENT

quote. This input can be helpful to the analytical team that will be putting the report together.

- **Regular Debrief Sessions.** Schedule daily debrief calls. Encourage all observers to attend. Stipulate that the purpose of these calls is for observers to share THEIR thoughts, not for observers to passively listen to what the moderator has to say. This will encourage them to take a more active role in observing.

Think of other ways that make it easy and "fun" for observers to actually observe. Remember that without observer feedback, the moderator is acting almost in a vacuum. Do what's needed to keep observers observing.

SECTION 7

⭐ Moderation

Participants have been recruited, the platform has been selected, the discussion guide has been finalized, and it's been uploaded to the system (for text-based methods). Now it's time to actually moderate. A lot can happen in an online focus group or interview, and moderators need to be prepared for a wide array of unexpected situations. This section is designed to help online moderators handle those situations with finesse.

• VIDEO | TEXT CHAT | BOARD •

TIP G-1: Use Names

Whether you are moderating a video chat, a text chat, or a discussion board, be sure to address participants by name. This personalizes the experience, and helps overcome the "distance" between the moderator and their participants. Calling somebody by their name in an online focus group is the equivalent of looking them in the eye in an in-person focus group.

When you want to call the group's attention to a comment made by a participant, mention the name of the participant who made the comment; it serves as a shout-out, a pat on the back to that person and helps others begin to remember who's who in the group.

The simple act of using their names makes them feel that they are being keenly listened to, which makes them more comfortable and can only help the data collection process.

108

7 | MODERATION

• VIDEO | TEXT CHAT | BOARD •

Tip G-2: Use Self-Introductions to Establish Rapport with Participants

Whether a focus group is conducted online or in-person, asking participants to briefly introduce themselves at the beginning is a standard part of beginning a focus group. A good moderator will take the opportunity to use this time to make participants feel comfortable and engaged. How the online moderator does this will vary depending on which online method is being used.

Video Chats

Moderator's Goal: Be a good host, demonstrate active listening.

- Even though participants' names will appear below their image on the screen, it's best to have each participant state their name because it may be pronounced differently than one might think (e.g., David might be pronounced Duh-*vid* instead of *Day*-vid). Don't offend participants by inadvertently mispronouncing their names.

- Based on their self-introduction, ask a follow-up question that 1) demonstrates that you listened to what they said and 2) will generate a brief response. For example: *"You said you like to travel. Where did you most recently travel to?"*

- Before letting another participant introduce themself, thank them and use their name before moving on. For example: *"Thanks, Sonia. Who would like to go next?"* Including their name personalizes the exchange.

Real-Time Text Chats

Moderator's Goal: Efficiently summarize

- Because everybody is able to "talk" at the same time in a text chat, and because it takes valuable time to ask follow-up questions of each participant in response to their self-introductions, the moderator can instead make a general observation or two about the group, after all self-introductions are posted. For example, *"Thanks for those intros. I see that we have people here from California (Megan) to Massachusetts (Ahmed), and many states in between. Thanks again for taking the time to be here. Let's move on to our first topic."*

Discussion Board

Moderator's Goal: Give everyone equal time

- Just as with video chats, make an observation or ask a follow-up question that demonstrates that you read their post. Since there's no rush, consider a follow-up question that might require a bit more time. For example: *"Thanks, Rebecca. Thanks for participating in this project. You mentioned having a young toddler. How old are they, and what growing-up phase are they going through these days?"*

Asking participants to introduce themselves isn't just to get baseline information from them. It's an opportunity to demonstrate that you are sincerely interested in what they have to say, and will be an active listener. That, in turn, will make them more engaged in your online focus group.

• VIDEO | TEXT CHAT | BOARD •

Tip G-3: Praise the Group—Not Individuals

A moderator's job includes keeping participants motivated and engaged. One way to accomplish this is by occasionally thanking them for their contributions during the discussion.

Within in-person discussions and in online video chats, moderators can offer praise verbally ("Good work, everyone") as well as non-verbally (via eye contact, a warm smile, and nodding one's head while a participant speaks). In contrast, during real-time text chats and multi-day discussion boards, the only way for the moderator to deliver praise is via text. Because the ways of offering praise in text-based groups is more limited, moderators should consider offering praise more often in those text-based methods. A good rule of thumb is to thank the group after each topic is completed; as a transition to the next topic "That was good work, everyone. Now, let's move on to my next topic."

Be sure that praise is distributed to the entire group—NOT to a particular participant. If some participants receive public praise, those who do

7 | MODERATION

not receive it may feel ignored or may feel that they are not as valued as those who receive the praise.

If the moderator feels compelled to offer individual praise in a text-based discussion, a safer approach would be to deliver that praise via private message.

• VIDEO | TEXT CHAT | BOARD •

TIP G-4: Minimize the Impact of Dominators

Just as with in-person focus groups, dominators—those who dominate the discussion by talking the most, frequently being the first to respond, positioning themselves as an expert, disparaging others' responses, etc.—can emerge in online focus groups as well. It is more difficult, however, for a dominator to have a negative impact in real-time text chats and in discussion boards, because they don't have the power of their voice and body language to dominate/intimidate, and because their responses can be ignored to a certain extent.

Dominators in Video Chats. If a dominant participant emerges during a video chat, there are a variety of tactics the moderator can use to minimize any negative impact on the productivity of the group.

- If a moderator notices one participant continuously offering the first response to most questions, the moderator can say, "[Name], you've gone first on many questions thus far. Let's let others be the first to answer the next few questions."

- In the case of excessively long responses, the moderator can interrupt the dominator with, "Please summarize your response quickly so we have time to hear from others."

- In the case of an "expert" in the group, publicly acknowledge their expertise and ask the expert to hold off and let others answer first, so that we're sure to hear their points of view.

- Remind the group (without singling out the dominator) of the need for all opinions to be freely expressed.

- If the platform has a private message feature, send one to the dominator, reminding them of the need for an open discussion.

- In the case of offensive remarks or language, warn the dominator that they must be civil or risk being removed from the group and receiving no incentive.

- While the need to eject a participant is very rare, if it happens, inform the group what you did and why, so that they don't wonder what happened to the missing participant.

Dominators in Real-Time Text Chats. When a respondent repeatedly posts excessively long responses, they may slow things down if the moderator courteously waits for them to finish each post. In that sense, they are bogging down the flow of the discussion. It's probably not their intention to do so, but they are inadvertently dominating the discussion. In this case, state publicly that quick, from-the-gut responses are most appreciated, and that if they have a long response, they should break it down into a series of short posts, using ellipses (". . .") at the end of each partial post to signal that more is coming.

- If the moderator is waiting too long for the last participant to post, they can say, "I need to move on." If the participant doesn't want to be left out, they will hopefully shorten their responses. As a follow-up step, a private message can be sent to the dominator, thanking them for their detailed responses, and encouraging them the "cut to the chase" with their responses so that they can keep up with the rest of the group.

- Another type of dominator in a real-time text chat is one who criticizes one or more other participants. In this case, a publicly posted reminder that ALL opinions are welcomed and that the purpose of the group is not to persuade, but to understand all viewpoints. If the dominator continues, a private message could be sent, stressing that disagreement is welcome, as long as it is done in a friendly way. The last course of action would be to threaten to remove the dominator from the group without incentive.

Dominators in Discussion Boards. In a discussion-board group, respondents can submit posts as long as they'd like them to be. But given the nature of discussion boards, they don't really dominate boards by taking time away from others.

7 | MODERATION

One way in which a discussion board participant becomes a dominator is by bullying other participants—ridiculing them. Or they may use offensive language. In either case, their behavior disrupts the collegiality of the board. The moderator has a variety of tactics to minimize the impact of this behavior.

- If the moderator is being attentive to the board, they can edit posts. If this is done, the participant whose post was edited should be informed of the action taken. They should also be told the rationale for the edit, and cautioned to avoid comments on the board that continue in the same vein.

- Another option is to refrain from editing the post, but post a reply (which will be seen by all), cautioning the participant that continued posts of that sort will not be tolerated.

· VIDEO ·

TIP G-5: Say "Cheese"

Realize that how you present yourself in a video chat can have an impact on your participants' impressions of you and their level of engagement in the discussion. Here are some tips to help you look and be your best:

- **Be Close.** Don't sit too far away from the webcam. Greater distance between you and the webcam may suggest an aloofness or shyness on your part. Being closer to the camera so that your face fills a quarter to a third of the screen suggests wanting to be closer to your group. Just as with in-person groups, lean in to give your participants the impression that you truly want to see and listen to them.

- **Reduce the "Blank Space" Above Your Head.** To maximize how much of you your participants see, position the webcam in a way that the top of your head is at the top of the frame. This will make it easier for participants to see any hand gestures you may use during your group.

- **Control the Lighting.** Be sure the light source is in front of you, highlighting your face. You don't want the light source behind you, creating a silhouette.

- **Place Webcam at Eye Level.** Most desktop monitors will be this way already, but laptops sitting on a desk often will have the webcam at neck level or lower, looking up at your face. Come across more professionally by elevating your laptop so that you are looking directly at the webcam, not down at it.

- **Look into Their Eyes.** Online moderators need to watch the screen to observe participants, but when they are looking at the screen, they are NOT looking at the webcam. While it may be difficult to do, at least occasionally shift your gaze to the webcam, especially when you are speaking, to give participants the impression that you are looking directly at them (even though you are actually looking away from them).

• VIDEO •

TIP G-6: Exercise "Crowd Control" in Video Chats

One of the challenges in video chats is getting participants to speak one at a time. If two or more talk at the same time, they "cancel each other out," rendering what was said as almost unintelligible.

COVID-19 lead to an explosion in the general use of video conferencing platforms, so many people now know that two or more participants talking at once can be an issue. They have learned to be more watchful about waiting for an opening to voice their comments.

Thus, there may not be a need to ask participants to raise their hands or click a button indicating that they would like to speak. In a very talkative group, the old-school method of calling on people to speak is a practical way to make sure we capture everything that participants want to say.

• VIDEO | TEXT CHAT •

Tip G-7: Limit the Use of Text Chat Within Video Chats

Most general-purpose video chat platforms offer text chat capability, allowing participants and observers to add text comments that can be seen by either one particular user (which the sender chooses) or everyone (participants, observers, and moderator). This capability is the equivalent of allowing participants to have side-conversations during in-

7 | MODERATION

person focus groups, which is what in-person moderators specifically ask participants to NOT do.

Ask participants to use text capability only when asked to do so (e.g., fill-in-the-blank exercise, short answer to a key question, etc.). This will keep everyone's focus on the main discussion, and will make the moderator's job much easier.

Note that this tip applies only to general purpose video chat platforms like Zoom. Video chat platforms that are designed specifically for qualitative research typically give the moderator control over whether participants have any text-chat capabilities. Also, the customized platforms are set up so that participants and observers cannot accidentally text each other.

· VIDEO ·

Tip G-8: Evoke More Engagement in Video Chats

In 2020, Bob Lederer's *Research Business Daily Report* video blog featured Susan Fader in one episode, sharing tips on how to inject more energy and interaction in video chats.* Here are some of the highlights:

- **Share your body language.** Moderators who typically gesture with their hands while speaking need to make sure their hands are visible to participants in online video chats. One approach is to sit further back from the webcam (perhaps even stand) to give your audience a fuller view of you. Another approach is to train yourself to keep your hands visible (move them up closer to your face) via the webcam. Enabling participants to see your body language will make them feel more connected to you and, by extension, to the rest of the group.

- **Say you want quick intros.** When asking participants to introduce themselves, give them a short time limit (30 seconds) to complete their self-introductions. A time limit for self-intros sets the stage for a fast-paced and energizing discussion. Don't sound a buzzer if some go over. The time limit is stated to give participants a goal to be short and to the point with their self-intros.

*https://www.youtube.com/watch?v=HOq1Dtsy_qM&feature=youtube

- **Invite participants to show and tell.** Before the group begins, ask participants to have on hand an item of theirs that is in some way connected to the discussion topic. Have each take turns showing their item and telling the group about it. Everyone likes to show a bit about themselves, and everybody likes to see what others are showing. This can be a good ice-breaker.

- **Turn over the reins.** Well after the group warms up, consider asking an articulate participant to take over the discussion for a few minutes. ("What do you think should be asked next?") Be there to help out if needed and take back the moderator role. The questions asked by temporary "co-moderators" may be insightful in and of themselves. Those who get chosen are likely to feel honored. If appropriate, it's fine to incorporate this exercise more than once in a discussion.

Always think of ways to add "zip" to online video chats.

• VIDEO •

Tip G-9: Take Advantage of "Virtual Easels" in Video Chats

In-person focus group facilities typically have easel stands, large-format pads, and markers available to moderators. Used appropriately, easels are an easy way to get the group to focus on a task at hand. For example, we might want the group to generate a comprehensive list of desirable attributes for a particular product or service. Seeing items added to this list can spark additional ideas, and having the list minimizes the same items from being repeated. Once the list is complete, it can be used as a springboard for further discussion, such as identifying the most important attributes on the list. Use of the easel can liven up the discussion because it is a diversion from a simple roundtable conversation.

Most video chat platforms (general-purpose platforms as well as platforms designed specifically for online qualitative research) make virtual easels available through the use of screen sharing. The platforms tend to call them "whiteboards," but I prefer to refer to them as virtual easels. If a moderator realizes in the middle of a discussion that an easel exercise would be helpful, it's easy to do. The moderator simply opens a

7 | MODERATION

new Word or PowerPoint page, shares their screen, and begins recording what participants add to the list. Pre-planning—setting up the page ahead of time, with a title—is certainly helpful, but not essential.

It's important for the moderator to announce in a video chat what they are about to do. Otherwise, participants may be a bit disoriented. Some examples:

"I'm about to open up a window to a blank page where I will list your responses to the next question."

"A new window will open on your screen. It's a description of an idea. Please take your time and read it thoroughly. When you are ready to talk about it, raise your hand."

Simply informing participants what's coming up and what they're about to see will make the group run more smoothly. Acting as a guide for participants will give participants a sense that the moderator is fully in control.

· TEXT CHAT ·

Tip G-10: Buddy Up for Data Collection

Moderating an online text chat can be unnerving, especially for first-timers. The three biggest stress-inducers for new moderators of real-time text chats are: 1) not being able to see and hear respondents, 2) discomfort related to setting the right pace and not being sure when all have answered question X before asking question Y, and 3) worrying about potential technical issues. All of these are ingredients for a stressful experience, even for experienced online moderators.

Use an assistant. One way to reduce stress while moderating is to make use of an assistant. The assistant's screen name is the moderator's name. What might an assistant do?

- Launch pre-loaded questions when directed by the moderator.
- Type in follow-up questions and probes as dictated by the moderator.
- Keep track of time and let the moderator know if they are on track or falling behind.

An assistant allows the moderator to focus solely on the discussion, strategizing about follow-up questions and NOT worry about typing.

Co-Moderate. Another stress-reducing option is to share moderator duties. Two moderators work side-by-side, either virtually or next to each other in the same room. If they are in separate locations, it would be good to have an open phone line between the two moderators because talking is faster than texting. Before the group begins, the two will decide who is moderating which parts of the discussion. The moderator who is "on break" can serve as another set of eyes on the discussion, offer suggestions to the "not on break" moderator about possible probes to ask, and monitor the activity level of each participant.

An assistant and a co-moderator will easily reduce the stress level for the moderator, enabling them to moderate more comfortably and confidently. As new online moderators gain experience, they may decide to give up these support mechanisms, or retain them as a best practice in their online text chat projects.

• TEXT CHAT •

Tip G-11: Deliver the Introduction in Real-Time Text Chats at a Relaxed Pace

In online text chats, it's standard practice for moderators to introduce themselves, explain the purpose of the discussion, describe how things will work, cover what's expected of the participants, and offer some guidelines. It takes time to go through these details, but it's time well-spent to address the many questions participants likely have when they enter a text chat.

Each moderator has his or her own way of handling this part of the discussion, and some moderators want to say more than others. Regardless of the time individual moderators take, observers (just as for in-person groups) might feel that the introductory remarks are a waste of time because they don't generate insights that meet the study objectives.

It's important to give every participant time to digest the moderator's full introduction in a real-time text chat, but the moderator may not know when participants are ready to see their next post in the in-

7 | MODERATION

troduction. One way for moderators to keep from posting their remarks too quickly is for the moderator to literally read each post aloud as it is posted. Read the posts at the same pace one would deliver them in an in-person group. Reading aloud at a comfortable (not rushed) pace will assure that participants of all reading speeds will be able to absorb each and every point.

Delivering the opening remarks more slowly helps set the pace for the discussion, and lets participants know that it will be more of a leisurely experience—not a frenetic one. Getting participants into this non-rushed rhythm will help them be more productive during the discussion.

• TEXT CHAT •

TIP G-12: Slow Down in Text Chats

One of the biggest challenges for chat-group moderators is establishing a comfortable pace and avoiding moving too fast through a discussion guide. This is especially difficult for first-time online moderators, but is sometimes experienced by more seasoned online moderators as well.

Without seeing respondents, moderators can easily fall into the trap of thinking that if we don't keep our online respondents constantly busy, we risk losing them. Moderators may also misinterpret the occasional "void of silence" in a text-based chat to mean that respondents are twiddling their thumbs, anxiously awaiting the next question.

For respondents to meaningfully interact with each another, we must provide an opportunity for them to first "hear" or "listen" to each other. In a chat environment, this means we need to give respondents plenty of time to read. Not just time to read, but to digest, ponder, and compose a response to other participants' posts.

If the moderator issues questions in a rapid-fire manner, respondents are left almost breathless. They barely have time to answer the moderator's questions, let alone engage in lively dialog with fellow participants. In this instance, there is a danger of turning what is supposed to be a group discussion into a set of simultaneous IDIs.

Of course, there are times when the moderator doesn't need much, if any, discussion beyond a quick answer to a question. Most times, however, a "meaty" discussion is desired. Moving too quickly may cause us to miss opportunities to delve more deeply into topics that are relevant to the project stakeholders.

A good rule of thumb is for the moderator to read ALL posts before asking the next question. If the moderator is having a hard time keeping up with the chat stream, chances are very good that the respondents aren't able to keep up, either. When that happens, the moderator needs to s-l-o-w down.

It's also a good idea to mention at the beginning of a chat that if it feels like things are moving slowly, it is purposely so. Tell participants that you want to give them the time to relax and actually "talk" to each other, not just the moderator.

When the moderator takes his or her time, respondents will be more relaxed and open with the moderator and each other. In the process, the moderator is more likely to unearth the nuggets of insight they and the other stakeholders seek.

• TEXT CHAT •

Tip G-13: Discourage Long Posts in Text Chats

In real-time text chats, the name of the game is speed. Once the moderator posts a question, participants need to read it, think about how to respond, then begin typing and post their response. Nobody wants to be the last to respond. As such, most participants provide quick, gut-level responses.

The moderator's job in a real-time text chat is to keep things moving at a brisk good pace, quick, but not so fast that participants are left breathless and don't have time to read others' posts and interact with each other. To foster short/quick responses, begin the discussion with questions that are easy to answer and will generate short answers. This helps set the pace for the rest of the session.

When participants send posts of roughly the same length at about the same time, they are in sync with each other. In a real-time text chat, having participants in sync with each other is a good thing. Most groups

7 | MODERATION

tend to naturally proceed with all participants in sync with each other. Occasionally, there will be a group in which one participant (or two at the most) will post much longer responses than everyone else.

Participants who habitually post long responses can slow the discussion because moderators tend to wait for all to answer a question before moving on to the next one. If participants are not in sync with each other, it can be a frustrating experience for the majority who are quicker. Fast responders are left twiddling their virtual thumbs while waiting for the "long-winded" participant to post a response.

Thus, it's important to rein in those who habitually post long responses or take a long time to post. Pick one or more from among the following options:

- **Add as a guideline at the beginning of the session:** *Answer as soon as you have read the question. Don't wait to read what others post before posting your own response.*

- **Say, as needed, during a session:** *If you have a lot to say, break it up into a series of shorter posts, using ellipses (". . .") to indicate that more is coming.*

- **Again, as needed during a session:** *If your posts tend to be longer than others' posts, and if you feel left behind, feel free to cut to the chase in your post.*

- **Send privately, as needed:** *I'm sorry to ask questions before you finish answering the previous question, but I need to keep moving. Your answers are just what I need. If they come late, I'll still be able to use your input. Thanks.*

By keeping everyone in the group relatively in sync with each other, the group will proceed at a comfortable pace. That will add to an enjoyable experience for everyone—participants, observers, and the moderator.

• TEXT CHAT •

TIP G-14: Wipe the Slate Clean

In real-time text chats, it's sometimes difficult to know whether all respondents have finished posting their answers to a question. If the Moderator asks the next question too soon, posts may appear that are actually responses to the *previous* question. In the moment it may be clear that it's a response to the previous question, because it appears too soon after the next question is posted. But that sense of timing is lost when reading transcripts later, especially if time stamps are only precise to the minute, not the second. In that case, there may be confusion when reading the transcript, and erroneous conclusions may be drawn if data are attributed to the wrong question.

An experienced moderator gets to know the rhythm of the group and can sense when it's appropriate to move on. For example, when a question requires only a short answer, and everybody's posted, it's a safe assumption that all are finished. But invariably, there'll be times when an additional comment is posted in response to a question *after* the next question is posted.

One way to keep things under control is to ask a "clean up" question before posting the next question. For example, after it appears that all are finished responding to a question, the Moderator can post, "I'm ready to move on. Are you?" Typically, all will quickly respond in the affirmative. If one or two respondents don't reply that they're ready, they are most likely still typing responses to the previous question. In that case, wait up to 10–15 seconds for them to finish posting. This delay slows things down a bit, but it keeps everyone in sync with one another, and makes understanding the discussion much easier. It enhances the user experience for all—the moderator, participants, and observers as well.

Another safeguard against confusion about which question a post belongs to is to make sure that questions are sequenced such that there would be no doubt which question a post belongs to. For example, don't ask "What do you like about Brand X?" and then next ask "What do you like about Brand Y?" Answers to the Brand X question may be posted after the Brand Y question is asked. However, asking "How familiar are

7 | MODERATION

you with Brand Y?" between asking for likes about Brand X and Brand Y will yield responses that would eliminate any confusion about which question a post belongs to.

· TEXT CHAT ·

TIP G-15: Deal Effectively with Difficult Participants in Text Chats

Because they can't be seen, it's easy for participants in a real-time text chat to blend into the woodwork (not fully participate), fail to reply to probes, insult other participants, or go overboard with foul language. Such behaviors create a less-than-optimal experience for all participants and as such are legitimate grounds for dismissal. (See Tip G-21 for further details on dealing with bullying behavior.)

A valuable feature of most text chat platforms created specifically for qualitative research is that moderators have the ability to remove problem participants from the group. In at least one platform, it's as simple as tapping a participant's name on a list and clicking the "remove" button. With those two easy steps, the participant is barred from re-entering the room.

That said, it's extremely rare for ejection to be required. In fact, text chat participants are more likely to leave the room of their own volition when they aren't enjoying themselves, see no value in continued participation, or for whatever reason don't want to be there. The key is to establish clear guidelines at the beginning, so that a participant cannot claim that they were unjustly removed from the room.

How can an online moderator minimize the need to eject a participant from the group? There are several things that the moderator can do, and they are presented here in order from mild/easy tactics to more aggressive approaches.

- **Manage expectations.** Share clear guidelines at the beginning of the session about how participants are expected to behave. See also Tip E-5.
- **Remind.** As needed, gently remind the group (without citing any specific participant) about the need to comply with a particular guideline.

124   MR. ONLINE'S PLAYBOOK

- **Get help.** Ask Tech Support to intervene. Tech Support sends a private message to the participant, explaining the issue and asking for their cooperation.
- **Private message.** Send a private message to the participant reminding them to cooperate.
- **Scold publicly.** Publicly reprimand the offender, which lets other participants know that the moderator is aware of the problem and is attempting to resolve it.
- **Threaten to remove.** Issue a final warning to the problem participant that they will be ejected and will forfeit their incentive if they don't immediately comply with the guidelines.

In all frankness, I cannot remember the last time I actually ejected a participant from an online chat. There have been less than a handful of instances when the last step was taken (threat of expulsion); in all of those rare cases the threat of the loss of the incentive seemed to be enough to get problem participants to miraculously become useful contributors to the discussion.

• TEXT CHAT | BOARD •

TIP G-16: Show Yourself

Moderators in any type of text-based qualitative research (real-time text chats or discussion boards) are literally faceless and run the risk of coming across as impersonal, perhaps even robot-like. One easy way for online moderators to come across as more human is to include a photo for participants.

- In any pre-discussion communications with participants, include your photo in the signature of the message.
- In a real-time text chat, post a photo of yourself at the beginning of the session, to show your participants who you are.
- If a discussion board allows photos to be uploaded as part of one's profile, moderators should include photos of themselves.
- If the discussion board platform does not allow photos as part of your profile, then just like in the real-time chat, include a photo of yourself in your introductory post. Better yet, if the platform allows

7 | MODERATION

it, include a brief video of yourself so that participants can not only see you but hear you as well.

Professional headshots are probably best because the background is neutral, and the focus is on your face, but a candid photo should work as well.

If you use a candid shot, be sure that it doesn't show anything which might conflict with the subject matter of your study. For example: If you were doing a project about outdoor grilling and you have a photo of you grilling, then great. However, if the study is sponsored by an outdoor grill manufacturer and your photo clearly shows that it is a competitor's brand of grill in the photo, avoid using that photo. And if the discussion is among grilling novices, refrain from using your personal grilling photo so as to not come across as an expert.

There are other ways moderators can present themselves as living, breathing humans, but one of the easiest ways is to include a photo, which leads us to the next tip.

• TEXT CHAT | BOARD •

Tip G-17: Be Human

By definition, text chats and discussion boards lack the "human touch" (being able to see and hear participants) of in-person focus groups or even online video chats. It's up to the online moderator to create a down-to-earth environment. The extent to which a moderator succeeds in creating a comfortable atmosphere can influence how engaged participants will feel and how productive they will be.

There are many ways to "humanize" these sessions. Here are some examples:

- **Share a photo or video.** As mentioned in the preceding tip, the moderator might choose to post a picture of him- or herself at the beginning of the session. A short, pre-recorded video is another option. Both options can be used in text chats or discussion boards.
- **Complete the circle.** After respondents introduce themselves, moderators can tell a bit about themself so that participants have a better impression of who they are.

- **Provide road maps.** Add "bridges" to transition from one question to another, or from one topic to another. *("You just told me what you like about this idea. Now, let's 'flip the coin' so to speak. What do you dislike about this idea?")*

- **Probe.** Demonstrate that you are listening. Where clarity is needed, ask for it. If information is missing, ask for it. If a provocative statement is made, acknowledge it. If humor is expressed, appreciate it.

- **Summarize.** Occasionally summarize what was heard before moving on. *("What you—as a group—seem to be saying is X and Y. Do I have it right?")*

- **Give thanks.** Don't wait to thank participants till the end of a session. As appropriate, give participants a virtual pat on the back to keep them motivated. *("Good work everyone. Thanks. Let's move on.")*

- **"Speak" naturally.** You should allow your speaking style to come across in text chats and discussion boards. One way to discover your style is to take the transcript from one or more of your in-person groups, extract only the moderator comments, and strip away the actual question that's already the guide. What's left is how the moderator typically ad libs in-person. Look for patterns, make note of them, and interject them into online guides.

- **Apologize for errors.** In the fast-paced text chats environment, online moderators might make small mistakes (spelling, grammar, or unclear questions). Acknowledge your humanness, admit mistakes to participants and move on. Here are some examples:

Situation	Solution (Moderator's Post)
Moderator interrupts the discussion by asking a question before participants finish responding to the previous question.	*"I thought everyone was ready to move on. I was wrong. Sorry about that."*
Moderator asks a question or follow-up probe that is unclear and confuses participants.	*"It looks like I didn't word that one very well. Hold on a moment while I re-phrase the question."*

7 | MODERATION

Situation	Solution (Moderator's Post)
Moderator refers to Participant X when they intended to refer to Participant Y.	*"Oops! I meant to say Participant Y."*
Moderator doesn't see or respond to a participant's question.	*"[Participant Z], I just noticed your question from earlier. I apologize for missing it."*

Admitting mistakes to participants or apologizing for small slip-ups shows humility. More importantly, it demonstrates that the otherwise faceless moderator is someone like them—someone who occasionally makes mistakes; it makes the moderator more human in the eyes of participants.

The more the moderator comes across as a person rather than a robot pushing questions out to respondents, the more enjoyable the participant experience will be and the more engaged your respondents will likely be.

· BOARD ·

Tip G-18: Act Like *The* Consummate Party Host

One of the biggest challenges for moderators of discussion boards is getting participants to interact with each other.

There are many ways to encourage interaction. One way is to play the role of a good party host (or friend) by introducing strangers to one another, helping to "break the ice." Participants will likely be asked to post their own self-introductions, but in the rush to get to the next question, they may not even read other participants' posts. Take advantage of those initial posts to create links between participants. Here are some possible moderator replies to self-introduction posts:

"Joe, did you notice that you and Bridget are both from Massachusetts?"

"Hillary, I notice that you are the fourth participant (so far!) with a 2-year-old son."

"Susan, you're the first from the West Coast to begin posting. I sense the Pacific time zone is waking up."

"Aha! We have two people in this group who both enjoy fly fishing—Brent and Kristen."

Pointing out what some participants have in common with each other helps create a bond between them, which will hopefully lead to some interaction between them as well. Just like at a party, some extroverts will reach out to others on their own. But many participants will appreciate having the moderator introduce them to each other.

This tactic can be used later in the discussion as well. For example:

"Brendan, it seems that you have the same point-of-view as Mark. Is that a fair assessment?"

"I see many different opinions on this issue. Look over what others have posted in response to this question thus far. Find at least one participant whose viewpoint is similar to yours and reply to their post, indicating which parts of their post resonate most with you."

While the above tips are most useful in discussion boards, they can also be used in text chats.

When a moderator points out to participants what they have in common with other participants, it shows that the moderator is really paying attention. It also creates and strengthens bonds between participants, which will not only result in a more engaging experience for them, but will hopefully get them to pay more attention and interact with each other.

• TEXT CHAT | BOARD •

TIP G-19: Refer to "Us" Rather than "Me" in Text Chats and Discussion Boards

In an in-person focus group, it's not uncommon for the moderator to say, "Tell me about X." As the moderator asks the question, they scan the room, making eye contact with participants around the table. The act of scanning the room while asking the question conveys to everybody that

7 | MODERATION

even though the moderator is saying "Tell *me*," what they really mean is, "Tell *us*" ("Share your story with the group").

Because participants don't see each other in a real-time text chats or discussion boards, moderators should stress that this is an interactive discussion with other participants, not just a series of simultaneous one-on-one interviews. One of the ways to do this in the online environment, especially at the beginning of a discussion, is to say "Tell *us* about X" rather than "Tell *me* about X." It's a subtle difference, that reminds each participant that they are part of an interactive group discussion.

• TEXT CHAT •

Tip G-20: Ask Participants to Refrain from Using Smartphones During Text Chats

Controlling cell phone use is more difficult in online groups than with in-person groups. At in-person focus group facilities, staff impress on participants the need to turn phones off (or at least silence them), and participants are usually very compliant. It's more difficult to impose this request in online groups, especially in text-based groups where we can't see or hear participants.

If participants are not explicitly asked to not use their phones during text chats, one or both of the following could occur:

- **Phones as a resource.** When asking an awareness question, participants may do a quick search to help them answer. Or, when asking for impressions of a company (or of a product or service category), they may do a search if they are unsure and want to sound knowledgeable to the moderator and to the group.

- **Phones as a distraction.** Participants may decide to read incoming texts or emails. They may even take time to respond to them. Both take their attention away from the discussion.

Neither of the above is what moderators want happening in their text chats. It behooves online moderators to ask participants to NOT use their phones to help them answer questions or to deal with matters outside of the discussion. Most participants will honor the moderator's request, especially if the reason for the request is explained to them. Thus:

- **This is not a test.** Participants should be reminded that what we need from them is what they happen to know. Impress on participants that there are no wrong answers. Reassure them that being unable to answer is a valid response.
- **Full focus is important.** Explain that time spent on their phone during the discussion slows down their reaction time to the question being asked and could result in having the group run overtime to cover all of the material. Remind them that there is a lot to cover in the limited time of the focus group, and that it's very important to be fully focused on the discussion at all times.

It's a relatively small request of participants to keep their phones out of sight, and they are generally happy to comply when they understand why the request is being made. Not all will comply, but if the number of those who don't comply can be minimized, or if the time they spend on their phones while participating in a group can be reduced, the group discussion will be more productive.

· TEXT CHAT | BOARD ·

Tip G-21: Halt Bullying Behavior in Text-Chats and Discussion Boards

Participants can't see or hear each other in real-time text chats and asynchronous discussion boards. No participant is in the physical presence of another, nobody can look another in the eye, and nobody needs to leave the facility with other participants. The anonymity they experience in these text-based online discussions empowers participants to be more likely to say exactly what's on their minds.

We certainly want from-the-heart responses, but sometimes participants will (whether intentionally or not) step over the line, making disparaging remarks about a participant if they don't like what that participant posts. Such disparaging remarks can be hurtful; they are a form of bullying, which can hurt the group process and keep it from being productive.

One might think that online focus group participants (strangers to each other) wouldn't be bothered by negative comments directed to them by another participant, but this is not the case. Many years ago, after receiving a private message from a participant asking why another participant was posting hurtful things about them, I began to include the following admonition when reviewing the guidelines: *"Disrespectful comments to others in the discussion will not be tolerated. Follow this simple rule: treat others as you would like to be treated. Feel free to disagree, but do so in a respectful fashion."* Since I began making that point at the start of every real-time text chat, I cannot recall ever having to call-out a participant for bullying behavior.

Bullying can happen in discussion boards, too. Because of the asynchronous nature of these boards, the moderator is likely to spot bullying posts before many other participants see it, and they can delete or edit offensive posts before they are seen by too many others. The participant whose posts have been edited or deleted should be informed of the action taken and the reason why, stressing the importance of having an open discussion without offending anybody. I can't recall having to do this more than twice in the past ten years. It's a rare event, but it certainly can happen.

The anonymity of text chats and discussion boards allows bullying behavior to occasionally surface. While the virtual environment allows participants to be more open than they might be in an in-person discussion, simple controls keep disruptive (bullying) behaviors to a minimum.

• TEXT CHAT | BOARD •

Tip G-22: Express Thanks

Participants in any qualitative research project want to be reassured that their contributions are appreciated. Doing so is easy in an in-person session and in video chats. Besides literally saying, "Thank you," moderators can use body language to convey appreciation; here are some examples:

- Leaning in to the table to show interest (in-person) or sitting close to the webcam (online)
- Smiling or nodding while listening to a participant
- Having eye-contact with individuals (See also Tip G-5.)

Body language can't be conveyed in online text-based methods, real-time text chats or discussion boards, so expressions of gratitude should be delivered more frequently to make up for the inability to give non-verbal cues.

In a text chat, thanks to the entire group *("Great work, everybody!")* should be delivered at least once every 30 minutes or so, or when moving on to a new topic.

In a multi-day discussion board, thanks to the entire group can be delivered at the end of each day. It wouldn't hurt to thank participants at the beginning of each day, too (e.g., *"Thanks again for all of your good work yesterday. Today, we shift our attention to ..."*).

Acknowledgments and thanks can also be given to individuals. There are many pretexts for extending a thank you to individual participants:

- Injecting humor into their posts
- Providing very detailed responses
- Engaging with other participants
- Asking good questions of others
- Having the courage to be an "outlier" (voicing a point of view that's markedly different from everyone else's)

Be careful about *publicly* thanking only a few participants too frequently, because those who aren't publicly thanked may feel less appreciated. One way around this is to thank individuals by *privately* posting thanks to them, or (in the case of an ongoing discussion board) sending them an email. Thanking an individual publicly is a useful way to signal to the entire group that you'd like to see more of a particular behavior, e.g., *"Thanks, Yves, for being the first to interact with others in the group. Hopefully more will follow your lead and interact with each other."*

See Tip G-3 for a related tip on praising individuals—not just thanking them.

7 | MODERATION

• BOARD •

TIP G-23: Strive for Omnipresence on Discussion Boards

Moderators can't be expected to attend to an online discussion board 24/7, but it's great if moderators can create the *illusion* of being on the board all of the time.

Over the course of a multi-day discussion board, most participants will get a sense of how engaged the moderator is with the discussion. That can, in turn, influence how engaged they will be. For example, if participants sense that the moderator only visits the board in the evening, then there is less incentive for them to visit the board in the morning or afternoon because they don't expect any new posts from the moderator at those times.

It is advisable to visit the board within an hour or two after a board launches, greeting each person after they respond to the self-introduction question. Those personal greetings show all participants that you are attentive to their participation.

It's also a good practice to visit the board within several hours after a new set of questions is launched. Do this to make sure that the questions are generating the type of feedback needed. Tweak the questions as needed to assure that those who have not yet answered will respond with more useful posts.

Moderators give the impression of always being online ("never sleeping") by visiting a board frequently (in general, at least once every 2–4 hours) and leaving signs (posts) that they have been actively "listening" to the discussion. These posts will likely be standard probes for further information or requests to clarify something. In the rare event that there is no need to ask probes, publicly applaud the group for the high-quality input you are seeing. Such "pats on the back" will not only let them know that you are paying attention to their posts, but it can spur them on to the board's finish line. Here are some examples of what you can post when there isn't much (if anything) to probe on:

- **Summarize.** "My understanding from the responses thus far is that _____. Tell me if I'm reading the group correctly."

- **Encourage.** "I really appreciate the time everybody is putting into their responses. I don't have any follow-ups for anybody at this time."
- **Acknowledge.** "It's clear to me where the group stands on this issue. Thanks."

When a discussion board is being used for one-on-one interviews, if you have no follow-up probes to ask, consider posting to the board (or send via email) a message that they are doing a great job. Again, show them that you are "listening" to them.

As the board progresses, the moderator will gain a sense of when participants tend to visit, whether they answer all questions at once or on multiple visits, and whether they are providing the level of detail needed. This information will help the moderator adjust their frequency and timing of visits to the board.

· BOARD ·

Tip G-24: Be Attentive to Discussion Boards in the First Few Hours After Questions Launch

Formal pre-testing doesn't happen much in qualitative research. Instead, qualitative researchers tend to rely on one or more best-practices such as these to assure that discussion guides are as good as they can be:

- Stakeholders provide feedback after reviewing each iteration of the discussion guide.
- Moderators read the discussion guide questions aloud to help determine if they "sound" right.
- The researcher asks a colleague or family member to act as "pre-testers" to assess the clarity of the questions.

Despite such best practices, once discussion board questions are launched, we sometimes find that a question may not be working as well as we had hoped (i.e., is not providing the insight we need). Usually, the problem stems from unintended ambiguity or missing information, and is easily corrected. It's best to detect these flaws and make revisions as early as possible after questions are launched (ideally within two hours after launch). The objective is to get the best data from as many participants as possible; allowing too many participants to respond to less-than-optimally-worded questions is counter-productive.

Be sure to pick a launch time for questions that fits the moderator's schedule. For example, a researcher on the U.S. Pacific time zone moderating a board with participants who are in the Eastern time zone might avoid launching questions at 6 a.m. Eastern. While 6 a.m. might be a good start time for the participants, 3 a.m. Pacific time is unlikely to be a good time for the moderator to begin moderating.

When a project includes more than one board using essentially the same guide, the process of being attentive to a board within two hours after questions are launched applies only to the first discussion board. Most (if not all) needed revisions are typically taken care of in the first board.

· BOARD ·

Tip G-25: Manage Your Time When Moderating Discussion Boards

Tip A-7 mentioned that a good rule of thumb is to expect to spend about four hours per day moderating a typical discussion board. That time can increase markedly when elements of the research design—number of participants, number of questions each day, number of suggested probes from Observers, etc.—are not tightly controlled. Thus, there are times when the moderating task becomes excessive. Here are some ways to manage this:

- **Create the illusion of being omnipresent.** Without actually moderating 24/7, give the impression of being at the board all of the time. There are two elements of this. First, make short but frequent visits to the board; moderate in blocks of 15–30 minutes. Second, be sure to visit the board multiple times throughout the day, from early in the morning until just before bed-time, to be there for the "early birds" as well as the "night owls." (See also Tip G-23.)
- **Take breaks.** With many short blocks of moderating time throughout the day, breaks naturally occur on data collection days. Once in a while, take an extended break (e.g., go out for a relaxing lunch or dinner, schedule a work-out, attend medical appointments, spend time with your family).

- **Use apps.** Most discussion-board platforms have an app that makes it possible for you to easily moderate from your phone, even while traveling or while out-and-about running errands.
- **Save analysis for later.** On the first day, focus on shaping participants' behavior—making sure they answer questions fully and clearly. Over time, if the shaping process is effective, participants will require less "nudging" so that the moderator can focus more on content. Don't feel compelled to work on analysis while moderating; there should be plenty of time for analysis after data collection is complete.
- **Consider an assistant.** Ask a junior colleague or an intern to monitor the board and alert you when you need to show your presence at the board. Another option is to work with a co-moderator. Each co-moderator can be responsible for taking a certain portion of each day, or moderation days can be traded.

A good discussion board moderator is a fresh moderator. Do what's necessary to be attentive while being fair to yourself as well.

• BOARD •

TIP G-26: Shape Discussion Board Participant Behavior on Day 1

Some discussion board participants aren't as diligent as others. They may give too-brief responses, forget to answer all parts of questions, fail to respond to follow-up questions, not be engaged with other participants, and in rare occasions may even copy others' posts. It's up to the moderator to spot these "bad behaviors" and take corrective action; doing so early and swiftly in the process gives participants the feedback they need to give the research team what it needs.

If the moderator doesn't take corrective action early enough, bad behaviors are likely to persist. And if otherwise compliant participants see others getting away with doing less, we run the risk of those bad behaviors spreading throughout the group, which, of course, threatens the value of the research.

There are two key things that online moderators can do on the first day of discussion boards to help cultivate good participant behaviors:

7 | MODERATION

- Ask for missing information as soon as it is spotted (e.g., *"Susan, it looks like you overlooked Part C of this question."*)
- Ask for clarification of ambiguous parts of posts (e.g., *"Ravi, the last statement of your post isn't clear. Please help me understand."*)

This type of feedback should be posted publicly, so that even those who are fully compliant can see that you (the moderator) are serious about needing full responses that are clearly understood. Public "admonishment" encourages the "good" participants to maintain their compliant behaviors.

Also, this feedback should be provided as soon as possible, ideally within a few hours of the errant post. Otherwise, participants may get the impression that the moderator isn't really paying too much attention.

Focusing on these participant behaviors on Day 1 is one way to shape participant behavior and assure that the best-possible data are collected. Taking care of these issues on Day 1 typically results in higher quality responses on subsequent days, which in turn will allow the moderator to focus less on compliance and more on the content of posts.

· BOARD ·

Tip G-27: Have at Least One Touch-Point with Each Discussion Board Participant

Every research participant—whether in-person, online, or over the phone—wants to feel valued. Certainly, some are motivated primarily by the financial incentive to participate and don't need any praise or other forms of encouragement from the moderator. But others like to know that they are doing good work, and that the feedback they are providing is appreciated.

It's easy to acknowledge individual efforts during in-person groups. Eye contact with a participant across the room, along with a smile and a head nod signals an affirmation of the individual. Also, a verbal "thank you" goes a long way toward making participants feel valued.

But what about online discussion boards, where we don't have eye contact, and we can't hear one another? Participants whose posts are ambiguous or incomplete should get a lot of moderator attention in the form of follow-up questions. But those who fully and clearly answer every question might not require any follow-ups; without those follow-up probes, they may feel ignored by the moderator and perhaps undervalued. *("I see the moderator posting follow-ups to others, but I'm not getting any feedback. Is there something wrong with my responses? Do I even belong in this group?")*

Some online moderators keep a tally of how often they engage with each participant. This helps them notice who is being left out of getting attention from the moderator. For those high-performing participants, here are several ways the moderator can easily give them some attention:

- **In-board.** Post a brief note of appreciation (private or public) in response to one of their last posts that day, thanking them for their clear and complete answers.
- **Email.** Send an email to the individual, acknowledging their contribution to the discussion and noting that while others have required follow-up questions, you appreciate not needing to do so with them.
- **Phone.** While rarely done, a phone call might also be worthwhile.

Do your best to have at least one touch-point with each participant within the first day or two of a discussion board project. Participants will be grateful for the virtual "pats on the back" they receive from you.

· BOARD ·

Tip G-28: Ask "TO EVERYBODY" Follow-Ups in Discussion Boards to Get Input from the Entire Group

In an in-person focus group or any real-time online focus group, the moderator may find an opportunity to go "off script" and ask a follow-up probe that isn't part of the moderator's guide. Most of the time, participants will know that the probe is for everyone to answer. If too few participants respond to the probe, the moderator will say, "I meant that question for everybody," to collect more input.

In a discussion board, these follow-up questions will appear as a reply to one participant's post. As such, it not obvious to participants whether everyone should respond, or if only the person who triggered the moderator's follow-up should respond.

To make it clear that all participants should respond, the moderator should preface the follow-up with **"TO EVERYBODY."** Note that the font is purposely larger, in all-caps, boldfaced, and in color to catch the participant's eye as they scroll down the page of a discussion thread.

To be most effective, the moderator should do the following:

- Announce at the beginning of the board that there may be TO EVERYBODY questions and that it is every participants' responsibility to find and respond to them.
- Explain that these TO EVERYBODY questions are easy to see.
- Be sure to use the font options to make the TO EVERYBODY question really stand out.
- Help participants out by telling them when these TO EVERYBODY questions are posted, and, even better, where these questions can be found. This can be communicated through an email blast to all participants, and there should not be more than one of these notices per day.
- Refrain from posting too many TO EVERYBODY follow-ups. Too many extra questions which everybody must answer adds to participants' work load, and moderators should not over-burden participants, especially if it's a full guide to begin with. (See also Tip E-19.)

· BOARD ·

TIP G-29: Challenge Discussion Board Participants to Interact with Each Other

One of the biggest struggles when moderating discussion boards is getting participants to "talk" to each other. Participants' natural inclination is to do only what they need to do to earn their incentive, which means responding to the moderator's questions only and ignoring other participants' posts.

More often than not, participants need to be coaxed to interact with others. There are many tactics that can be used to accomplish this. Here are the steps to make it work:

1. **Set Expectations.** Let participants know during recruitment that there will be other participants, and that they are expected to interact with them.

2. **Remind.** When login information is sent, tell them once again that they are expected to read and react to others' posts.

3. **Challenge.** During the introduction on the first day of the board, issue a challenge to them to reply to at least two other posts made by others each day. It's a small/easy request.

4. **Cheer.** The first time (or two) that you witness a participant interacting with another, call it out. Post a public reply to the interacting participant, prefaced with "TO EVERYBODY" (to maximize visibility). Call out the name of the participant who interacted, and thank them for demonstrating the type of participation that you hope to see more of as the board continues.

5. **Clarify.** In that same "cheering" reply, remind everybody that you don't expect them to read and reply to every post that others make. Tell them that when they strongly agree or disagree with a post, when a follow-up question of their own pops into their head, or they feel like building on somebody's post, they should follow through with that gut reaction.

6. **Remind Again.** On subsequent days, remind them of the "challenge" issued on the first day.

Notice that there's no requirement for participants to interact with each other. So, the "challenge" comes across as encouragement to have fun and be more involved with each other, rather than an edict that must be followed. If we can entice them to do some minimal interaction with each other, it will hopefully become a habit, and they will end up interacting more than they otherwise would.

· BOARD ·

TIP G-30: Require Discussion Board Participants to Fully Participate to Earn the Incentive

One way to maximize the amount of data collected from participants in a discussion board is to instruct them that they need to answer ALL questions to receive their incentive. In other words, present an all-or-

7 | MODERATION

nothing deal; if they don't answer all questions, they don't receive any incentive. If they want their incentive, they will be more likely to stay with the board and not drop out.

But what if a participant drops out after the first or second day of a three-day board? There are instances when unanticipated things happen (illness, unexpected work assignments, death in the family), preventing some participants from being able to fulfill their obligation to the project. *If a participant appears to put in a good-faith effort to finish but isn't able to, and if their (incomplete) data will remain part of the analysis, I recommend paying a partial incentive.*

For example, if a participant completes only the first day of a three-day board, give them up to a third of the incentive. Even though they don't get the full incentive, they get credit for the partial effort they put into the project. This will come across as fair to them and leave them with a good feeling about the project. Remember that when they dropped out, they were told to not expect any incentive. The next time they may be recruited for another discussion board study, they will not be thinking, "Well, I got stiffed the last time I got sick and couldn't finish the assignments, so I'm not going to bother with this one. I'll decline the invitation to participate."

· BOARD ·

TIP G-31: Coax Discussion Board Participants to Answer Follow-Up Questions

In multi-day discussion boards, each participant is likely to be asked several follow-up questions. Some will be asked more follow-up questions than others, depending on how clear and complete their responses are. In our experience, anywhere from a quarter to one-half of participants will not respond to the follow-ups and will need to be nudged to do so.

One way to encourage response to follow-ups is to begin each day with a reminder to respond to any follow-up questions from the previous day.

Another way to maximize responses to follow-ups is to ask participants to "clean up" toward the end of the last day. The text we typically use goes like this:

"In a 3-day discussion board like this, it's easy to overlook some of my follow-up questions. With that in mind, please do me a BIG favor. Starting at the beginning, click on each of the questions and scroll down to be sure you've answered all follow-ups. Don't forget to answer all of the TO EVERYBODY questions, too! Once you're sure that you have answered all follow-ups, say so here, then move on to my final questions."

A participant could say "yes" and move on to the next question, whether they have (or have not) actually answered all follow-ups. Thus, they could lie. Most, however, will not want to lie. They will dutifully go back to the beginning and respond to any unanswered questions, especially if they have been told from the start and reminded that complete answers to all questions (including follow-up) must be answered to earn the incentive. Coaxing participants to answer all follow-ups results in a more complete/robust data set.

P.S. I wish platform providers can come up with an automated way for the software to identify unanswered follow-up questions and provide this info to participants and the moderator.

· BOARD ·

Tip G-32: Excuse Unproductive Discussion Board Participants Only as a Last Resort

In an online discussion board, the best participants show up and respond to questions several times each day, they engage with other participants, they give thoughtful and complete responses, and they dutifully respond to all follow-up questions directed to them.

Typically, there may be one or two participants in a board who do not show up every day, who post the shortest responses possible, who give no indication that they are reading others' posts, and who refuse to answer any follow-up questions from the moderator. Their contribution to the discussion is lackluster at best.

Assuming that the moderator's expectations of participants have been clearly laid out, when "better" participants notice less-productive participants, they may justifiably ask, "Why should I put so much time and energy into this discussion when some of the other participants ar-

7 | MODERATION

en't doing nearly as much as me?" That sentiment might undermine the integrity of the board.

The moderator should be on the lookout for these less-productive participants and take actions to minimize their potentially negative impact. Here is a three-step process that could be taken:

- **Step 1: Private Message.** Phone or send an email to less-productive participants, letting them know that they need to be more productive. Do this as early as possible, to give them ample opportunity to "catch up." (This can be done by the moderator, the recruiter, or the project manager.) Most of the time, this private message approach is all that's needed.

- **Step 2: Public Message.** If Step 1 doesn't work, the moderator can then publicly post a reply to one (or more) of the less-productive participant's posts, stressing that they need to be more engaged or risk being removed from the group and losing their incentive. This signals to others that this misbehavior is noticed and is not acceptable.

- **Step 3: Possible Removal.** In the rare case that Step 2 doesn't work, the moderator or project manager may consider removing the less-productive participant from the group. However, before doing so, answer this key question: "If I remove this participant, am I willing to remove all of their data?" If the answer is no, then perhaps the less-productive participant should not be removed.

It is important to deal with these less-productive participants as early as possible, so that if a replacement is needed to meet commitments about minimum number of participants to complete the project, there is sufficient time to make that happen.

· BOARD ·

Tip G-33: Notify Discussion Board Participants About Follow-Up Probes Only in IDIs

Many (if not all) online discussion-board platforms give moderators the option of sending email notifications to participants whenever a follow-up question from the moderator is asked. This saves the participants time. They don't have to search for any follow-up questions from the moderator.

This is a wonderful feature for IDIs (in-depth interviews, or one-on-one interviews), but what about interactive group discussions, where interaction among participants is desired? One could justifiably argue that participant reliance on email notifications about follow-up questions from the moderator will diminish their likelihood of reading others' posts, which will in turn decrease their likelihood of interacting with others. For that reason, consider NOT sending alerts about moderator follow-ups in discussion boards. We want participants to routinely interact with each other. They are more likely to do so if they are "forced" to look for follow-up moderator probes on their own.

Email notifications about follow-up questions from the moderator have the potential to turn what is supposed to be an interactive group discussion into a set of simultaneous IDIs.

· BOARD ·

Tip G-34: Don't Panic if Show Rates are Low When a Discussion Board Launches

The research team is frequently on pins and needles on the first day of a discussion board. Even though recruits have promised to participate, one never knows how many will show up, or when will they begin to show up. This is the nature of boards.

Here's a checklist to make sure you've done everything possible to assure that a low show-rate on the first morning isn't a signal that something's wrong.

- Keep reminding participants beforehand about the launch date/ time of the board.
- If a participant is recruited more than 3 days before the board's launch, get participants to re-confirm their participation 1–2 days before the launch.
- Send an announcement to all participants notifying them that the board is open.
- Be sure respondents understand that daily participation is required.

7 | MODERATION

- Double-check where participants reside. The time zone they are in can impact when they should be expected to appear at the board.
- Consider making participation prior to noon on the first day a screening requirement. Alternatively, consider offering a small bonus for the first x number of participants who begin posting before a specified time on the first day.

If all of the above are checked off, and show rates are worrisome through the early afternoon, choose one of the following tactics:

- **Moderator action.** Send another email notice (or text) to participants who've not yet begun posting at the board. Be up front with them. *("The discussion board has been open since [time], but only [Y number of people] have logged in and begun posting. Please begin posting soon, because it's beginning to worry me and the project team. If you don't think you'll be able to participate till much later, please let me know.")*
- **Recruiter action.** Ask recruiters to phone or text participants, encouraging them to log on soon. Sometimes a phone call (even if it's voice message) will prompt participants to act. A phone call is preferred because it is personal, while emails or text messages are less personal and easy to disregard.

If toward the evening of the first day, show rates are still very low, consider re-opening the recruitment process to replace the no-shows. Because boards typically go on for days, there is some time to find replacements.

SECTION 8

☆ Analysis

Once all of the data are in, it's time to summarize. Analysis of qualitative data collected online is the same as analysis of data collected in-person. Still, technology is available to make parts of the analytical process a bit easier. Hopefully one or more of the following six tips will spark some interest.

• BOARD •

TIP H-1: Hold Daily Debriefs During Discussion Boards

One of the biggest challenges with discussion boards is getting observers to actually observe. Even though they may have the best intentions to fulfill their observer duties, other things (unexpected phone calls, meetings, and assignments) can get in the way. While we might ask them to block time on their calendars for observing the board, it's so easy to say, "I'll get to that later," if an interruption arises; the problem is that they end up never reclaiming that observer time.

One tactic to foster more client observation is to schedule a daily phone debrief with the entire observer team. These should be short (15–20 minute) meetings, where the moderator can report on the status of the board (participation levels, quality of responses, etc.) and offer some very high-level insights. These meetings are also an opportunity for observers to provide feedback on whether the discussion is on track, to suggest additional probes that might be beneficial, and to decide whether any changes need to be made to the guide in subsequent days.

To *effectively* participate in a debrief session, observers must have some familiarity with the content of the discussion that day. They don't want to show up for a debrief meeting unprepared; being unprepared could make them look bad in front of their peers (and their manager.)

8 | ANALYSIS

Knowing they are expected to be present and actively participate in the debrief encourages them to make sure they spend at least some cursory time at the board. It may not be the amount of time we would like them to devote to observing, but it's better than no time at all.

Another approach to consider is to "divide and conquer" the topics. In other words, if two topics are being addressed on a given day, one observer can take responsibility to at least skimming the content of the first topic and another observer can read through the posts for the second topic. This is a way to "share the wealth;" it requires less work of each individual observer.

· BOARD ·

Tip H-2: Embrace the Volume of Data from Discussion Boards

Text-based discussion boards are known for generating lots of data. It's not unheard of for a single 3-day discussion board with 12–16 participants to yield a transcript that's over 100 pages long. This might seem overwhelming, but there's a bright side to this.

Cleaner Transcripts. Despite the volume of data from a discussion board, there are several advantages discussion board transcripts have over transcripts from in-person groups or video chats.

- **Well-organized.** All responses are neatly organized under each question.
- **More data.** Everyone answers, not just a few.
- **No confusion.** The data are clearer. There are no disappointing transcriber notes like "participants talking over one another" or "unintelligible."
- **Multiple views.** Want a traditional transcript in Word? You got it. Prefer to get it in an Excel spreadsheet to group participants in particular ways? That's an option, too.

Opportunities to jump-start the analytical process. Most platforms provide tools to help with analysis. Taking advantage of these features while the group is going on will save time in the analysis phase. In addition, the discussion can include ways for:

148   MR. ONLINE'S PLAYBOOK

- **Flagging quotes.** As a discussion board ensues, the moderator will know a good quote when they see one. These can be marked and easily retrieved later on.

- **Coding.** Many researchers will code the data after the analysis. Many discussion guide platforms include the capability of coding the data in the platform, as it comes in and is read by the research team. There's no need to wait till the board is complete before initiating the analysis.

- **Getting participant input.** Periodically (no more than daily), the moderator can post a short top-line summary recapping what was learned, and ask participants to react to it. Participants appreciate being involved in the process, and it provides some feedback on initial hypotheses that are uncovered.

Despite their heft, discussion board transcripts are easier to deal with than most other transcripts, making the analytical process less overwhelming.

· BOARD ·

Tip H-3: Provide and Get Feedback on Mini-Analyses During Discussion Boards

Those who have moderated multi-day discussion boards are often faced with the issue of *"How do I deal with all of this data?"* There are no magic tricks to make the analysis of online qualitative data easy, but there are things that online moderators can do to make the process feel less daunting.

One way to lighten the analytical load is to compose a short summary at the end of each day of the board, present it at the beginning of the next day of the board, and ask the group how well you encapsulated what the group said. Most will likely give the summary a stamp of approval, which is of course reassuring. Some participants may take issue with some parts of the summary, and offer more insights; in that case, the moderator gets some "bonus" data.

The summary should take no more than 10–15 minutes to prepare. At this point in the data collection process, it can be based on gut-level re-

8 | ANALYSIS

actions to what participants are saying. One approach is to limit yourself to 3–5 key take-aways from that day of activities. This little exercise has several benefits:

- For the **Moderator,** it jump-starts the analytical process. The sense of being overwhelmed by the amount of data at the end of the data collection period should be mitigated.

- **Observers** get the equivalent of a top line summary each day, which brings them up-to-speed if they were unable to spend as much time observing as they would have preferred. Observers may also weigh-in on the accuracy of the summary, which will help the report-writer shape the analysis.

- **Participants** see that they are genuinely being heard. They also appreciate the opportunity to clarify some fine-points that the moderator may have either overlooked or misunderstood.

Thus, with a relatively small investment of time each day, everybody wins.

Most importantly, once the boards are complete and the analytical process begins in earnest, hopefully the mini-reports prepared through the process will provide some structure to both the analysis and report writing.

· VIDEO | BOARD ·

TIP H-4: Take Advantage of the Power of Video for Reports

Video chats and some discussion board platforms provide us with opportunities to amplify the "voice of the customer."

Video Chats. Most in-person focus groups get recorded using a stationary video camera behind the mirror in the observation room. It's rather boring footage. The camera may not capture a speaker's face, such as when a participant sitting near the moderator addresses a participant at the other end of the table, in which case we may see nothing more than the back of the speaker's head.

In contrast, video chats allow us to capture all participants' full faces. If video clips are desired to include in the report or to create a short clips reel that supplements the report, clips from video chats are more useful.

Full-on views of participants speaking can have more impact because they can make it seem (almost) that each participant is speaking directly to the viewer.

In addition, some video chat platforms allow the researcher to extract the video of just the person speaking in a focus group. This brings that participant (and their voice) front and center in the report or in a reel. If used well, that video can be most impactful—potentially more impactful than just a quote included in the report.

Discussion Boards. Some discussion board platforms have video capabilities as well. Here are two suggestions for taking advantage of that capability (where it exists):

- The moderator can record an introductory video for participants as the first thing they see when they log on. It's more personal and engaging.

- As a closing question, ask participants to summarize their thoughts and feelings on an issue, encapsulate what they thought about the concept being discussed, or sharing some final advice to be passed on to the study sponsor. Limiting the amount of video responses from participants to just one or two questions will save on analytical time and will make editing film clips and assembling a short reel less onerous.

• VIDEO | TEXT CHAT | BOARD •

Tip H-5: Take Advantage of Tools to Streamline Parts of the Analytical Process

There are a number of tools available to make the analysis and reporting phase of qualitative projects a bit less onerous. These tools are especially suited to online qual projects, but may be applicable to in-person projects as well:

- **Word Clouds.** Several types of exercises (e.g., fill-in-the-blank, brand attributes) tend to generate long lists of words and phrases. Dropping that data into word cloud software could provide quick visual depictions of how participants think. Those word clouds can then be included in reports.

- **Heat Maps.** Some platforms offer mark-up exercises for stimuli. Typically, participants would digitally flag a particular part of the stimuli that appeals to them (or that they dislike), and attach a comment to that flag. The software usually produces heat maps, which help the researcher see which parts of the stimulus receive the most positive and negative attention. These heat maps can also be included in reports.
- **Segmentation Analyses.** Many online platforms feature a polling function. Some platforms also have the capability of linking individual participant screener data to poll responses, which can provide insights about segment differences.
- **Video Editing.** Editing video clips from video chats or from video responses to discussion board questions can be a fun/creative process, but it's a time-consuming task. Some platforms include machine transcription of video responses, which, when tied to the video, makes editing and creation of reels easy. Researchers use transcripts to highlight the text they want to clip, and the software will extract portions of video that were highlighted in the transcript.

The above examples are by no means an exhaustive list of capabilities. Be on the lookout for others. Some may be available in-platform for no additional charge. Other tools are available separately and may be free or may have a cost.

• VIDEO | TEXT CHAT | BOARD •

Tip H-6: Explore the Feasibility of Using Data Analysis Software

Some qualitative researchers (both online and in-person researchers) love the analysis part of the research process, while others hate it. Some online qualitative methods exacerbate the love-hate feelings researchers have regarding the analysis task.

- **Drinking from a fire hose.** Transcripts from online discussion boards are typically 3 or more times the length of in-person focus group transcripts. The sheer volume of data can be overwhelming.
- **Incorporating video in reports.** The rapid adoption of video chats due to COVID-19 has created an opportunity to include video clips

in reports, adding to the list of responsibilities that researchers should tackle in their work.

How is analysis typically done?

Whether based on online or in-person methods, most seem to use a brute force method of analysis, taking copious notes while watching videos, listening to audio recordings, or reading transcripts.

Another option is to use data analysis software tools. Some have been around for decades. None are free. A partial list of these software tools includes Delve, NVivo, Reduct, and Relative Insight. New tools are likely to come on the market, so it's a good idea to do a web search on "data analysis tools for qualitative research" to get a full up-to-date list.

None of these tools absolves the researcher of doing some necessary "dirty work." The researcher (or someone working with the researcher) must still "teach" the software what to look for. This typically involves a coding process, taking a look at all responses to a question or issue and systematically classifying all responses.

As this book is being published, ChatGPT is a hot topic. Many wonder whether it can reliably and effectively assist in any part of the in-person or online qualitative research process. ChatGPT may be helpful in providing a preliminary analysis of research results based on transcripts. But the results should not be blindly accepted as accurate. ChatGPT itself cautions users to scrutinize results to make sure they are valid. As time goes on, it will be interesting to see the extent to which ChatGPT is actually useful, and the degree to which it is adopted by researchers.

If used properly, data analysis software can provide a more thorough and accurate catalog of findings. Through this accuracy and thoroughness, the tools can help uncover patterns in the data that might otherwise be overlooked. Perhaps most significantly, the software can help spot differences between sub-segments of those included in the research.

For those who wince at the idea of "traditional" manual data analysis, data analysis software tools may represent a way to streamline the process.

Mr. Online's Tipsheet

PAGE	TIP	TITLE	VIDEO	TEXT CHAT	BOARD
1 | THE FUNDAMENTALS					
1	A-1	Be a Champion for ALL Qualitative Methods	X	X	X
2	A-2	Don't Fear Online Qual	X	X	X
3	A-3	Think of Video Chats as the "Kiddie Pool" for New Online Moderators	X		
4	A-4	Watch Your Language	X	X	X
6	A-5	Recognize that Moderating Online is Different than Moderating In-Person	X	X	X
8	A-6	Know When One Text-Based Method Should be Used Over Another		X	X
9	A-7	Realize that Moderating Discussion Boards Takes a Lot of Time			X
10	A-8	Understand the Pros and Cons of Text Chats vs. Video Chats	X	X	
12	A-9	Know What All-Purpose Video Chat Platforms Offer (and Don't Offer)	X		
14	A-10	Know the Differences Among Discussion Board Platforms			X
15	A-11	Exercise Caution When Using DIY Discussion Board Platforms			X
16	A-12	Be Familiar with Which Tools Are Available on Which Platforms	X	X	X
17	A-13	Know that Sampling Sources Are Increasing	X	X	X

PAGE	TIP	TITLE	VIDEO	TEXT CHAT	BOARD
18	A-14	Remember that Sensitive Subjects Work Well Online	X	X	X
20	A-15	Consider How Increased Reliance on Mobile Devices Impacts Online Qual	X	X	X
21	A-16	Keep Up with the Latest Developments in Online Qualitative Platforms	X	X	X
22	A-17	Be Prepared for Investment Requirements in Community Panel Management		X	X

2 | SELLING ONLINE QUALITATIVE

PAGE	TIP	TITLE	VIDEO	TEXT CHAT	BOARD
24	B-1	Tout the Ever-Increasing Pool of Online Consumers	X	X	X
25	B-2	Highlight More Authentic Participant Feedback	X	X	X
26	B-3	Propose Side-by-Side Designs for Online Qualitative Skeptics	X	X	X
27	B-4	Schedule a Demo for Prospective Clients		X	X
28	B-5	Self-Fund a Project for Future Demo Purposes	X	X	X
30	B-6	Take Advantage of Platform Branding Options When Appropriate	X	X	X
31	B-7	Know that Online Qual Is Not Necessarily Less Expensive than In-Person	X	X	X
32	B-8	Calculate Professional Services Costs Carefully	X	X	X
33	B-9	Watch the Time			X

3 | GENERAL DESIGN CONSIDERATIONS

PAGE	TIP	TITLE	VIDEO	TEXT CHAT	BOARD
35	C-1	Determine if Online Is Appropriate	X	X	X

PAGE	TIP	TITLE	VIDEO	TEXT CHAT	BOARD
36	C-2	Consider Mixed-Method Qualitative Approaches	X	X	X
37	C-3	Cap Text Chats at 90 Minutes		X	
38	C-4	Provide Ample Time for Breaks Between Real-Time Video and Text Chats	X	X	
39	C-5	Conduct International Discussions in Participants' Native Language			X
40	C-6	Use Apps That Participants Are Comfortable With	X	X	
41	C-7	Consider Video Chats for Research with Children	X		
42	C-8	Manage the Number of Discussion Board Participants			X
43	C-9	Schedule Discussion Boards Consecutively			X
45	C-10	Establish Capacity Limits in Discussion Boards			X
46	C-11	Determine if the Layout of a Discussion Board Platform Will Be Suitable			X
48	C-12	Anticipate Whether Break Days in Discussion Boards Would Be Helpful			X
49	C-13	Opt for Real Names Whenever Possible	X	X	X

4 | RECRUITMENT

PAGE	TIP	TITLE	VIDEO	TEXT CHAT	BOARD
51	D-1	Consider an Automated + Manual Recruitment Process	X	X	X
52	D-2	Manage Respondent Expectations During Recruitment	X	X	X
54	D-3	Relieve Any Respondent Anxieties	X	X	X

PAGE	TIP	TITLE	VIDEO	TEXT CHAT	BOARD
54	D-4	Decide Which Devices Participants Should Use to Effectively Participate	X	X	X
56	D-5	Reinforce the Need to Use Particular Devices to Participate	X	X	X
57	D-6	Maximize Show Rates in Real-Time Chats		X	
58	D-7	Harness the Power of Reminder Calls	X	X	X
60	D-8	Coach Video Chat Participants on How to be Helpful	X		
62	D-9	Protect Client Intellectual Property	X	X	X
63	D-10	Plan Carefully for Online Focus Groups with Employees	X	X	

5 | DISCUSSION GUIDES

PAGE	TIP	TITLE	VIDEO	TEXT CHAT	BOARD
65	E-1	Appreciate the Value of a Thorough Warm-Up	X	X	X
67	E-2	Mix It Up		X	X
68	E-3	Use Polls to Help Participants Focus	X	X	X
69	E-4	Beware of Client-Provided Discussion Guides	X	X	X
70	E-5	Provide Clear Guidelines in Text Chats		X	
71	E-6	Combat Multi-Tasking by Participants in Text Chats		X	
72	E-7	Right-Size Real-Time Text Chat Discussion Guides		X	
73	E-8	Narrow the Scope of Questions in Real-Time Text Chats		X	
74	E-9	Get Participants to Answer Multi-Part Questions in a Single Post		X	

TIP SHEET

PAGE	TIP	TITLE	VIDEO	TEXT CHAT	BOARD
75	E-10	Control When Participants See Others' Posts in Real-Time Text Chats		X	
76	E-11	Schedule Breaks as Needed in Real-Time Chats		X	
76	E-12	Offer Tips about Length of Posts in Real-Time Text Chats		X	
78	E-13	Strive for Unaided Responses, as Needed		X	X
79	E-14	Be Transparent When Seeking Unbiased Responses		X	X
80	E-15	Use Text Formatting and Layout Options to Help Communicate		X	X
81	E-16	Know the Pros and Cons of Discussion Guide Uploading Options		X	X
83	E-17	Manage Discussion Board Participant Expectations When a Board Launches			X
84	E-18	Include Guidelines in Online Discussion Board Introductions			X
85	E-19	Be Respectful of Discussion Board Participants' Time			X
87	E-20	Right-Size Discussion Board Moderator's Guides			X
89	E-21	Spread the Work Evenly			X
90	E-22	Give Titles to Discussion Board Topics and Questions/Activities			X
92	E-23	Use Question Sets in Discussion Boards			X
93	E-24	Specify How Much Depth Is Needed in Discussion Board Responses			X
94	E-25	Use Masked/Uninfluenced Mode Sparingly			X
95	E-26	Allow Discussion Board Participants to Interact with Each Other			X

PAGE	TIP	TITLE	VIDEO	TEXT CHAT	BOARD
96	E-27	Use This Checklist to Maximize Participant Interaction in Discussion Boards			X
97	E-28	Require Interaction in Online Discussion Boards, As Needed			X
98	E-29	Prevent Discussion Board Participants from Skipping Questions			X
99	E-30	Set the Bar High to Go Deeper			X
100	E-31	Take Advantage of Video Capabilities of Discussion Board Platforms	X		X
101	E-32	Leave Room for Extra Questions on the Last Day of a Discussion Board			X
102	E-33	Beware of Backgrounds in Video Chat Platforms	X		

6 | OBSERVER MANAGEMENT

PAGE	TIP	TITLE	VIDEO	TEXT CHAT	BOARD
104	F-1	Control Observer Requests During Real-Time Chats		X	
105	F-2	Make the Real-Time Text Chat Observation Process Engaging		X	
106	F-3	Strengthen the Online Discussion Board Observation Experience			X

7 | MODERATION

PAGE	TIP	TITLE	VIDEO	TEXT CHAT	BOARD
108	G-1	Use Names	X	X	X
109	G-2	Use Self-Introductions to Establish Rapport with Participants	X	X	X
110	G-3	Praise the Group — Not Individuals	X	X	X
111	G-4	Minimize the Impact of Dominators	X	X	X
113	G-5	Say "Cheese"	X		

TIP SHEET

PAGE	TIP	TITLE	VIDEO	TEXT CHAT	BOARD
114	G-6	Exercise "Crowd Control" in Video Chats	X		
114	G-7	Limit the Use of Text Chat Within Video Chats	X		
115	G-8	Evoke More Engagement in Video Chats	X		
116	G-9	Take Advantage of "Virtual Easels" in Video Chats"	X		
117	G-10	Buddy Up for Data Collection		X	
118	G-11	Deliver the Introduction in Real-Time Text Chats at a Relaxed Pace		X	
119	G-12	Slow Down in Text Chats		X	
120	G-13	Disencourage Long Posts in Text Chats		X	
122	G-14	Wipe the Slate Clean		X	
123	G-15	Deal Effectively With Problem Participants in Text Chats		X	
124	G-16	Show Yourself		X	X
125	G-17	Be Human		X	X
127	G-18	Act Like *The* Consummate Party Host			X
128	G-19	Refer to "Us" Rather Than "Me" in Text Chats and Discussion Boards		X	X
129	G-20	Ask Participants to Refrain from Using Smartphones During Text Chats		X	
130	G-21	Halt Bullying Behavior in Text Chats and Discussion Boards		X	X
131	G-22	Express Thanks		X	X

PAGE	TIP	TITLE	VIDEO	TEXT CHAT	BOARD
133	G-23	Strive for Omnipresence on Discussion Boards			X
134	G-24	Be Attentive to Discussion Boards in the First Few Hours after Questions Launch			X
135	G-25	Manage Your Time When Moderating Message Boards			X
136	G-26	Shape Discussion Board Participant Behavior on Day 1			X
137	G-27	Have at Least One Touch-Point with Each Discussion Board Participant			X
138	G-28	Ask "TO EVERYBODY" Follow-Ups in Boards to Get Input from the Entire Group			X
139	G-29	Challenge Discussion Board Participants to Interact with Each Other			X
140	G-30	Require Discussion Board Participants to Fully Participate to Earn the Incentive			X
141	G-31	Coax Discussion Board Participants to Answer Follow-Up Questions			X
142	G-32	Excuse Unproductive Discussion Board Participants Only as a Last Resort			X
143	G-33	Notify Discussion Board Participants About Follow-Up Probes Only in IDIs			X
144	G-34	Don't Panic if Show Rates are Low When a Discussion Board Launches			X

8 | ANALYSIS

PAGE	TIP	TITLE	VIDEO	TEXT CHAT	BOARD
146	H-1	Hold Daily Debriefs During Discussion Boards			X
147	H-2	Embrace the Volume of Data from Discussion Boards			X

PAGE	TIP	TITLE	VIDEO	TEXT CHAT	BOARD
148	H-3	Provide and Get Feedback on Mini-Analyses During Boards			X
149	H-4	Take Advantage of the Power of Video for Reports	X		X
150	H-5	Take Advantage of Tools to Streamline Parts of the Analytical Process	X	X	X
151	H-6	Explore the Feasibility of Using Data Analysis Software	X	X	X

r

About the Author

Jeff Walkowski
QualCore.com Inc.

Jeff Walkowski is the principal of QualCore.com Inc., a consulting firm providing traditional and online qualitative research services to a wide ange of industries including health care, financial services, automotive, and information services. He was schooled as a quantitative specialist and entered the industry in the 1980s as a statistician. He later discovered his talents as a moderator and evolved into a qualitative specialist by the mid-1990s.

Jeff's specialty is online qualitative. He has conducted over 700 online sessions (real-time text chats, video chats and multi-day discussion boards); he has spoken about online qualitative at conferences in North America, Europe, and Asia; and he has published articles on the subject. Jeff co-chaired the Online Qualitative Research Task Force of the Qualitative Research Consultants Association, co-edited *Qualitative Research Online* (Research Publishers LLC, 2004), and in 2002 co-founded the Online Moderator Training Institute to help traditional moderators adapt their skills to the online world (www.OnlineModerator.com).

Jeff thrives on variety and has mastered most qualitative approaches. Thus, he is equally adept at conducting research in person, by phone, or over the Internet. He enjoys conducting in-depth interviews, mini-groups, and focus groups. His practice includes a healthy mix of consumer and business-to-business projects. He has interviewed a wide range of people, from grade-schoolers to senior citizens, stay-at-home moms to company presidents, truck drivers to engineers, and new parents to physicians.

He has international experience was well, having provided on-site supervision of qualitative research projects in London, Paris, Rome, Milan, Hamburg, Moscow, Mumbai, Hyderabad, Bangkok, Shanghai, Beijing, and Tokyo.

Jeff holds an MBA from Southern Methodist University, an MS (Educational Research) and a BA (Psychology) from Southern Connecticut State University, and has been a faculty member of the RIVA Training Institute since 2000. In addition, he authored the qualitative marketing research course for the University of Georgia's and MRII's Principles of Marketing Research online certificate program, which launched in 2019.

Jeff served on the Board of Directors of the Qualitative Research Consultants Association (QRCA) from 2002-2006 and served two terms as President of that international organization. In addition to being actively involved in the QRCA, he is also a member of the Insights Association.

Jeff is an active volunteer. Since 1997 he has been a volunteer cook for Clare Housing—a Minnesota non-profit that provides housing for those with HIV/AIDS. He is an interviewer for the Red River Rainbow Seniors Oral History Project based in Fargo, North Dakota. He has been a juror for the Fargo Film Festival since 2011. He also leads his Minneapolis neighborhood's "Welcome Wagon" program.

He can be contacted at: 17 Washburn Avenue S., Minneapolis, Minnesota 55405; 612.377.3439; Jeff.Walkowski@QualCore.com.